THE DIRECTION OF LITERARY THEORY

Also by Steven Earnshaw

POSTMODERN SURROUNDINGS (*editor*)
POSTMODERN SUBJECTS/POSTMODERN TEXTS
(*co-editor with Jane Dowson*)

The Direction of Literary Theory

Steven Earnshaw

St. Martin's Press
New York

THE DIRECTION OF LITERARY THEORY
Copyright © 1996 by Steven Earnshaw
All rights reserved. No part of this book may be used or reproduced in any manner whatsoever without written permission except in the case of brief quotations embodied in critical articles or reviews. For information, address:

St. Martin's Press, Scholarly and Reference Division,
175 Fifth Avenue, New York, N.Y. 10010

First published in the United States of America in 1996

Printed in Great Britain

ISBN 0-312-15914-5 (cloth)
ISBN 0-312-15915-3 (paperback)

Library of Congress Cataloging-in-Publication Data
Earnshaw, Steven.
The direction of literary theory / by Steven Earnshaw.
p.   cm.
Includes bibliographical references (p.   ) and index.
ISBN 0-312-15914-5 (cloth). — ISBN 0-312-15915-3 (paper)
1. Criticism.   I. Title.
PN81.E16   1996
801'.95—dc20   95-47334
                                                                CIP

For my mother and father

Contents

		Page
	Acknowledgements	viii
1.	Introduction	1

Part I

2.	Making the Author Function: The Wives of Thomas Pynchon and Paul de Man	21
3.	'Murder Case Man's "Threat" to Shoot Teddy Bears': Intention in Literary Theory	36
4.	Well and Truly Fact: Postmodernism and History	59
5.	About Value	82

Part II

6.	Thanks for the Theory	107
7.	Alterity: Martin Buber's 'I-Thou' in Literature and the Arts	119
8.	Impossibility Fiction? IF Only …	135
9.	Despair, Enchantment, Prayer: A Conclusion	150
	Appendix: 'Impossibility Fiction' Conference – call for papers	160
	Notes and References	162
	Bibliography	173
	Index	177

Acknowledgements

I would like to thank Deborah Madsen for her guidance through some very difficult terrain.

Many thanks are due to the following for their willingness to debate the issues, and their interest in the project: Jon Begley, Catherine Burgass, Mark Rawlinson, Clare Hanson, Katharine Cockin, Philip Shaw, Danny Cordle, Peter Smith and Nick Everett.

Thanks go to Ray Osborne and Jim Parkin for their constant reminders of 'the reading experience'.

Personal thanks to Laurence Redmond and Geoff Tait for an ongoing no-nonsense approach to the whole affair.

1
Introduction

The Direction of Literary Theory emerges in the context of what is commonly called a crisis for English Studies. This apprehension is somewhat misleading in that the subject remains as popular as ever with students in schools, colleges and higher education. Although the so-called crisis primarily relates to a critical debate amongst academics, the issue can be seen to have much wider consequences as ideas are promoted and placed under practical scrutiny in the spheres of education and public comment. It has been the case that it has had a mixed reception in education, and, more often than not, been misrepresented and ridiculed (not without some justification) in the public domain. The debate focuses upon issues such as the nature of English and what can be said to constitute Literature, gender, race, ethics, value, politics, aesthetics, psychology ... the list is as long as it can be exciting. It might be said that this is also a sign of healthy interest rather than the imminent collapse of literary studies. This book is concerned with what is at the heart of the crisis – literary theory. Dealing with theory, it will also in the latter chapters attempt to relate the work back to what continues to keep the subject as buoyant as it is – student interest.

Literary theory has mushroomed since the 1970s, although twentieth-century precursors can be found much earlier in the work of the Russian Formalists in the 1910s and 1920s. The first guide book for literary theory is, claims Patrick Parrinder, Wellek and Warren's *Theory of Literature* of 1949.[1] In that book the two main parts are split into 'intrinsic' and 'extrinsic' criticism. This is indicative of the history of theory to date – its momentum has been generated by the ding-dong battle played out by advocates of one system or the other. We can say that the dialectic began earlier than even Wellek and Warren's book, in that Saussure's structural (intrinsic) approach to language was challenged by the work of Voloshinov in the 1920s and his insistence upon the sign as a social fact (the extrinsic approach).

To deal with literary theory at its most crucial level it would therefore seem appropriate to tackle this opposition head on. To begin with the two antithetical camps can be described as follows. The one camp comprises approaches, methodologies and theories broadly classed as sociohistorical (extrinsic), whereas the other camp consists of approaches, methodologies and theories which I shall term 'immanence-based' or 'immanence-orientated', by which I mean activities that take 'the text itself' as the object to be worked upon, irrespective of contexts such as backgrounds of authors and reception histories. This second mode often attracts such epithets as 'transcendental' and 'ahistorical'. The former (extrinsic) group consists of critical and theoretical processes which regard knowledge as contextually based, such as certain types of feminist critical activity, those in the line of marxist/materialist enterprises, and any theories or approaches which regard literature in a historical context. The latter category of 'immanence-based' roughly covers the formalist/structuralist/poststructuralist axis. The book, in its first part, assesses the possibility of mediating between the two camps. This is deemed necessary since the history of literary theory has been underwritten by the mutual incompatibility of these two opposing camps. A theoretical solution, or at least clarification, is therefore desirable.

Yet immediately there is a problem of method in that books of this nature are expected to demonstrate a logical structure, something of the nature of an initial proposal (as above), proceeded by argumentation and a conclusion of sorts. Also, I want to solve theoretical problems using the tools of theory. But what if the tools themselves are inadequate? (But then a bad workman always blames his tools!) So, whilst the book attempts to find a mediation between the oppositions that would enable theory to move beyond the divide, and attempts to maintain the requisite linear argumentative thread which can give a rational, reasoned argument that builds cumulatively chapter by chapter, there are tensions involved that require the book to make a major move away from such a straightforward progression.

Introduction

The received idea of a commitment to a rational argumentation in keeping with the presuppositions of theoretical endeavour needs some attention. Certain issues *can* be resolved, or at best elucidated, using the tools and reasoning provided by theoretical discourse, yet at certain points theory simply becomes inadequate to the task. Although the original proposition is framed as a theoretical problem, solutions, it will transpire, are both theoretical and *non*-theoretical. Non-rational theory can feed back into the dictates of rational theory, or we might simply describe it as non-rational theorising (that is, theory that cannot exclude the imaginative, the emotional, the existential). To accommodate this difficulty the book is therefore split into two parts. The first part works within the putative bounds of literary and critical theory and takes the thinking there as far as it can reasonably go. The second part shifts perspective in that it is philosophical, both in a technical and an everyday sense, and non-rational. It disputes theory's self-validation from an (acknowledged) untheorisable position outside of theory's circumscription, taking up some of the same problems already expounded in the first part, but in a new environment.

The 'structure' of Part I can be best understood as the collection of a number of different ways of looking at the same object (or process). This object/process we receive already designated as 'Literature'. Part I looks at it according to the concerns of what have often proved the most intransigent of problems for literary theory current and past: 'the author', 'intention', 'postmodernism', and 'value'. The following quotation from Nietzsche illustrates the potential advantages of such a method:

> All seeing is essentially perspective, and so is all knowing. The more emotions we allow to speak in a given matter, the more different eyes we can put on in order to view a given spectacle, the more complete will be our conception of it, the greater our 'objectivity'.[2]

Of course, there are theoretical objections to the methodology of Part I. The first would be that there is an assumption that Literature is a fixed, concrete object that we can take in our hands and turn around as we please, giving ourselves the complete view which can lead to full comprehension. As such the metaphor of different gazes on a single object might seem a hopelessly inadequate analogue, since we cannot 'see' 'Literature' as we can 'see' a statue. Literature simply does not exist in a like manner in the phenomenal world. Yet say for instance that we choose to study an abstract concept like 'power'. We observe that a parent slaps a child and note that the punishment is accepted by both parties. We decide that this is an example of 'power' even if we have no fully satisfactory definition of it. We might say that 'power' is a necessary fiction which allows us to get a grip on events in the phenomenal world. And because of similar difficulties that have to be faced when we begin to talk about Literature, the difficulties associated with its ontological status and the lack of any complete or even half-adequate definition, we might approach the concept of Literature in a like manner and regard it too as a necessary fiction, consisting of observable phenomena which exist in some relation to the necessary fiction; just as 'the slap' exists in some relation to 'power', so 'a novel' exists in some relation to 'Literature'.

A related objection is that in capitalising the term itself I have in some way accepted its status as a special object, when, in the light of poststructuralist criticism, the boundaries that separate one type of text from another, most specifically Literature ('the best', that is, the most 'good' or most 'beautiful' novels, plays, poetry) from any type of written material which might be called 'literature' (pamphlets advertising car-boot sales or religious meetings, for example), have been 'problematised' or eroded. A presumed similar erosion is provided by the challenge to 'the high cultural canon' whereby Literature, once regarded as separate from popular culture, is now regarded in the same way as anything else that might form part of that semiotic system – films or adverts, for example – and not as some special practice.[3] However, as the book proceeds, it will become evident that the use of a capital 'L' is justified, not only by the above analogy with 'power', but also on a number of other grounds. To pre-empt such objections even at this early stage, it is useful to look at James Kirwan's excellent *Literature, Rhetoric, Metaphysics: Literary Theory and Literary Aesthetics* in some detail since it so cogently tackles the same riddles as we are faced with here. This is how Kirwan's book opens up the problem:

> The question this work sets out to answer is, simply, 'What is literature?', and, perhaps more pertinently, 'What can literature be for criticism?'
> What I include under the heading of this 'literature' to be defined, will emerge as I go on.[4]

His introductory wish is simply to position his argument. He does this by answering objections to his project in order to prevent it 'being damned even before its prosecution'.[5] He divides the objections into two camps, 'that there is no such thing as literature to define', or that, for the sake of literature, 'literature should not be defined'. Kirwan goes on to analyse and refute the following possible conceptions of Literature: 'family resemblance' (Wittgenstein); the argument for 'the institutional concept of literature', which Kirwan mockingly sees as making a claim for itself to be 'irrefutable – or at least will be, as soon as everyone has agreed to its truth';[6] placing literature 'sous rature'; Hirsch's intuitionism, that is, everyone knows what it is anyway (the second type of objection). Rather than simply repeat the working-through of the dismissals here, solely to endorse them, I urge the reader to seek out Kirwan's book.

After he has treated the problem of 'what is literature?' negatively, Kirwan proceeds to lay his own cards on the table. First he states: 'It is the very lack of agreement about what is to be called literature that makes literature a stable object within the critical tradition.'[7] This approach, unfortunately, can hardly help us, since it is proposing that the concept 'literature' has only managed to survive by being all things to all people, and thus sounds rather like an extreme version of Hirsch's intuitionism. However, Kirwan usefully goes on to say:

> All the objections to the attempt to define 'literature' that I have here considered (including Hirsch's) arise, paradoxically enough, from the belief that no such definition has yet been found. I would assert on the contrary, that what literature is has been implicit in all the writing that has surrounded the word,

that all writers on literature have been right, even when they contradicted one another. This on reflection is inevitable; for to assert otherwise one would have to begin from the truly metaphysical question 'Is "literature" literature?'.[8]

I am grateful to Kirwan for this clarity and repeat his line of argument to forestall similar objections, although one would want to ask Kirwan: if 'what literature is has been implicit in all the writing that has surrounded the word' then is there not some common denominator, some deep structure or algorithm, that would account for such a statement? However, Kirwan and this book part company when he describes on what basis *Literature, Rhetoric, Metaphysics* is to proceed: 'I have begun with metaphor because, as will emerge, metaphor provides the best model of literature *from an aesthetic point of view*'.[9] We cannot resort to that luxury, since the very category 'aesthetic' has been challenged by various parties, especially by post-Marxists such as Tony Bennett. (The book does broach the issue of metaphor, but in a different context, in the chapter 'Impossibility Fiction'. Metaphor, as is shown in this chapter, is just as intractable as the other concerns of Part I.) Nor can it prejudge the issue by rejigging the question 'What is literature?' as 'What can literature be for criticism?', although I take Kirwan's point. The derived question is neither a necessary condition of all responses to 'What is literature?', as might be supposed, especially by such a work as this, nor can it be the dominant guideline for a possible solution. Part II implicitly shows that this leap from 'literature' to the *study* of literature (as criticism or theory) is at best in bad faith, and at worst incommensurate with 'the nature of' Literature, just as is the leap to 'metaphor'. Rather than ask the question 'What can literature be for criticism?' I am more inclined to ask 'What can literature be for pedagogy?' and subsume criticism under that rubric, and this indeed does inform much of Part II. But neither of these two transformations of the original question 'What is literature?' suffices for our purposes, and Part I strives to avoid any such starting-point as 'metaphor' by maintaining its notion of different perspectives without a predefined object, just a necessary fiction.

A second objection to the methodology of Part I might be raised against the creation of the subject/object distinction, with Literature positioned as the object about which we can ask questions and know. Pushed far enough it becomes a question of the nature of knowledge itself. 'In the current postmodern climate' would serve as an appropriate introductory phrase for all the epistemological hazards involved here. What kind of knowledge can I have, and in what kind of framework? If I construct my object in a particular way, am I not destined to ask corresponding questions and receive corresponding answers that are already implicit in the very construction? In other words, so the argument goes, any objective knowledge is always precluded because there is no point 'outside' the object from which to study it. But this is only an objection if I claim that I can have absolute knowledge – an ideal that itself has increasingly come under attack. The argument is familiar to poststructuralism and its critics in the domain of textual decidability: if a text's meaning is not completely (absolutely, objectively) decidable, due to the intrinsic nature of language and writing, then, it follows, poststructuralists et al. would argue, that meaning is subject to the play of infinite slippage. This is an argument that has become untenable, as such books as Raymond Tallis's *Not Saussure*[10] and Christopher Norris's *What's Wrong with Postmodernism*[11] persuasively show, and has begun to veer towards some kind of compromise which agrees to a sliding-scale of objectivity that ranges from the possible/probable to the impossible/improbable. This is the approach the book takes, and once again I refer the reader to the notion of looking at an object – 'literature' – from a number of different perspectives with the intention of gaining a greater objectivity (there is an analogous argument with the use of multiple narratives to understand historical events – see the chapter 'Well and Truly Fact: Postmodernism and History'). A corollary of this approach would be one that proceeded along 'pragmatist' lines. Pragmatism is charged with a particular interest because its solutions are always already there in the sense that its definition of 'truth' is a question of what something does in the world, not what is intrinsic to it. However, 'pragmatism' can also be charged with being part of, or at least implicated in, the 'current postmodern climate', with its strong antifoundational rationale, and is dealt with in that chapter. The move from Part I to Part II however, as already suggested, initiates a different approach to knowledge which redefines what might be accepted as knowledge within the discourse of Literature (and the Arts in general). It takes that part of the quotation from Nietzsche which is most likely in the current climate to be overlooked – 'the more emotions we allow to speak' – very much into account.

A third objection to Part I might take the metaphor of different gazes on the same object and argue that, although the object is viewed from a number of perspectives, the viewer still views with one set of assumptions, that is, sees in one particular way, no matter how many different angles are used or considered available. Furthermore, it might be objected, to claim that there is no single sustained line of argument to the book is to be either disingenuous or critically vacuous. But is it not possible that a critic or theoretician has the power to take on and use views not necessarily conducive to his or her own? One positive legacy of poststructuralism has surely been this recognition that the notion of criticism and theory as parasitic upon, and secondary to, primary imaginative writing has been, if not overthrown, severely questioned. Although I do not hold with this supposed breakdown of disciplinary boundaries (again see the chapter on postmodernism) 'imagination' is not the exclusive domain of 'primary' material. It is possible to 'imagine' – to what extent is debatable, but nevertheless it is feasible – seeing through other eyes. Perhaps we should talk of the 'critical' or 'theoretical imagination'. The general impression I get from students is that Literature can help readers to broaden their horizons by virtue of seeing through others' eyes.

The philosophical rider to 'seeing' and Literature would be Sartre's work upon 'imaging' and 'perception' as summarised by William Ray in *Literary Meaning: From Phenomenology to Deconstruction*:

> the perceived object always exceeds the consciousness of the perceiver: no matter how many aspects of that object we perceive in any given instant, we know it possesses an infinite reserve of other possible relations, both to other objects and between its own elements.[12]

Yet this is pure speculation on Sartre's part since there is no way of knowing if an object *can* always and endlessly escape the gaze or interaction of the viewer or interpellator. Is it not nearer the mark in any case that something that is not capable of being circumscribed, that is infinite, can not be an object? Even if Literature is to be described as event or process rather than object, it still remains circumscribable, although once again it depends upon the discursive field initially prescribed. It is true that one person can never see all six sides of a cube at the same time, but nevertheless it *is* possible to form a complete picture and to know it as a cube, and this is how Part I may be presumed to proceed as the logical attempt to find this mediation. Part II, because it finds no *a priori* reason to proceed in such a logical manner, takes Sartre's description more on its own terms and discusses this notion of 'the always out of reach' nature of Literature, particularly in the chapter on 'Impossibility Fiction'.

Simply using the concept 'text' is positionally charged and can be said to predetermine the argument. David Lehman makes this point when discussing deconstructionists:

> *Text* ... seems strategically chosen. It is, for one thing, a great leveler, since it serves equally well to describe the label on a soup can and an ode by John Keats – and reinforces the notion that these various 'texts' are equal in importance.[13]

Equally, if I describe a piece of writing as 'a poem' or 'a novel' I seem to have prejudged the issue. Is this mere pedantry? (it feels like it) or is it a matter of the highest importance (it seems like that too, as when Barthes claims: 'The language we decide to use to define the text is not a matter of indifference, for it is a part of the theory of the text to plunge any enunciation, including its own, into crisis').[14] The problem again lies with whatever I choose to define as 'Literature'. To say that 'a novel' exists in some relation to 'Literature', whereas a soup can label does not, begs the question of what my definition of 'Literature' is. This problem is addressed by examining the proposed and desired (by some critics) 'collapse' of literary studies into cultural studies at the end of the chapter on value.

An objection related to the problem of 'text' could be made by arguing that I have played off 'text' against 'context' in my use of the terms 'immanent' and 'sociohistorical', and have therefore situated 'text' in the manner that Lehman claims deconstructionists and other structuralists/poststructuralists have. However, I do not regard the relationship between 'textual' and 'immanence-based', 'contextual' and 'sociohistorical' approaches as necessarily symmetrical. There is scope, as suggested above and as shown in the chapter on 'value', to redefine 'text' in a way that does not automatically orientate written material into a particular discursive field.

Another objection that could be raised is that I have promoted a straw target to attack in that neither pole of the oppositions is ever as extreme as the book makes out. To answer this I would point to William Ray's book already mentioned which surveys literary theory and finds not radical discontinuity but sees the whole field underwritten by a shared 'common ground, which is to be found in a pervasive notion of literary meaning underlying theoretical and critical programs from phenomenology to the present'.[15] At the heart of this notion of meaning there always seems to have been 'at least two meanings' with respect to literature, a

> historically bound *act*, governed by a particular intention at a particular moment, and permanent textual *fact*, embodied in a word or series of words whose meaning transcends particular volition and can be apprehended in its structure by any individual possessed of the language.[16]

Thus, far from being a straw target, the polar opposites of immanence and transcendence (along with their many correlates) are at the very heart of the project of literary theory so far, as I suggested in the opening comments. Ray would see the work of Fish, Barthes and de Man, as attempting to outmanoeuvre the problematic, through belief and transcendence (Fish), *jouissance* (Barthes) and irony (de Man), but illustrates how they do so either at the cost of self-contradiction (which is a re-enactment of the initial dialectic), or what amounts to a forgoing of epistemology in favour of enjoyment of the text, or a kind of acceptance of the infinite regress such a wavering between the two extremes involves.

But I would argue that these are not mediations so much as attitudes to be adopted based on personal responses, and as such do not work through the polarisation but leave it very much intact. Still, it is worth bearing in mind that an attitude may be as valuable as a theory.

Ian Hunter, like Ray, also identifies a version of the two camps as having been central to generations of theorists and critics. He gives a genealogical (Foucauldian) account of the emergence of literary education to demonstrate that English did not develop to address some pre-existing problem of man's nature – a problem framed as how to reconcile an innate aesthetic (transcendent) sensibility with the circumstances of everyday social reality (contingency). Instead, he argues that the system developed 'piecemeal',

> emerging in the autonomous sphere of 'social welfare'; a sphere formed when traditional techniques of individual pastoral surveillance were redeployed in a new machinery of government aimed at the 'moral and physical' well-being of whole populations. It was in this domain that popular education could take shape as an apparatus of moral supervision. And it was as the privileged inheritor of this apparatus – not as the mediator of culture and society – that modern literary education first came into being towards the end of the nineteenth century.[17]

Hunter's is an excellent account that avoids the reductive arguments of literary education as a crude ideological tool, whilst showing just how it does fit into the network of state power and the peculiar position English studies has grown into. To accept Hunter's argument as a full explanation for the central dichotomy would, however, mean *confining* the issues to pedagogical ones. Hunter's avowed project is to reconsider 'the relation between the idea of culture and the machinery of government'.[18] To this end literary education provides him with a most salient example. As such Hunter skews what might be said about our relation to Literature. I would counter that just as Literature (the Arts) does not exist or is not produced (created) so that theory can be written, nor is its *raison d'être* to be taught. Whilst I am perfectly happy to concede Hunter's genealogy as it relates to literary education in the form of 'English' and the particular (no doubt 'peculiar') way

Literature within that field has been determined, I do not believe that it resolves or even diffuses the antithetical divide. Hunter's achievement is to make us aware of just how our discourse is and has been shaped with respect to English and the theory that attends to it. Yet, to use an analogy, the etymology of a word can only go part way to telling us about current usage and current meaning. To describe English as a tool of social machinery does not eliminate: (1) the current apprehension of the 'two camps' divide; (2) the fact that 'contingency' and 'transcendence' has a history and significance far wider than Hunter's exemplary history; (3) our problematic relationship to Literature (Art) is not restricted to the pedagogic sphere. How this broader significance of Literature beyond the limitations of both 'theory' and 'pedagogy' is manifest is dealt with in the later chapters, particularly those in Part II.

Fault can be found in that I have, to a large extent, predefined the discursive field of Literature by confining it to difficulties with 'meaning'. Other initial positions might have been 'pleasure' or 'value'. This is quite true, but I think for ease of approaching the whole topic this question of starting point is not of such great consequence, since, as will become clear, a look at any particular one of these categories would involve the discussion of the others.[19] This is indeed the case with the book – 'value' is taken up as a separate chapter, and the question of 'pleasure' occurs repeatedly in Part II. It will also be noted that the question of 'value' splits into another version of these two antithetical camps, absolute value on the one hand (immanence) and relative value on the other (contingency).

There is an objection to the very existence of such a book as this in that in trying to conceptualise the process of meaning it turns that very 'process' into what can be seen as its antithesis, 'structure'.

> Even viewed dialectically, [the process/structure of meaning] cannot be controlled by a concept because it cannot be reduced to a structure, and because the event of conceptualization assumes a further grounding structure – and thus puts into question its own 'conclusion'.[20]

This can be taken as an objection to the grounding of the book, since if I am dealing with a process – which the word 'mediation'

I am using undeniably suggests – but using structure (the structure of this book) to define it (to define its meanings or implications), any conclusion must needs be compromised. So would my concluding mediation be process or structure? In the sense that a book is a finished item, even if it acknowledges itself as part of an ongoing debate/dialectic/dialogue, it must be viewed as structure. It could be argued that it is process in that it is only in existence, or has its mode of existence, in the process of meaning production (by you, the reader). This is truly a vicious circle, in which the book is doomed to tackle the problem – let us say a mediation between poetics and hermeneutics, a mediation between process and structure – with the problem itself as the only tool, an attempt to solve the problem *with* the problem.[21] The book is structural and calls for the description of a process it can only define in structural terms. To extrapolate from Ray, to believe in the possibility of describing the mechanism or engine of the process would be to assume 'a further grounding structure'. A way out of this might be to regard the book in some way as 'history'. At this point I would merely speculate on the nature of a book going from introduction through to conclusion as re-enacting an historical analogue of cause-and-effect, of going from the origin to the telos (both structure and the re-enactment of the event, the process of the book coming into being). Should the book bear the traces of its own history, that is, and for example, should it give a narrative of its own development/change? Or should it maintain the analytic chronological sequence of propositional knowledge, which in effect creates the illusion of a synchronic gesture which can organise all the material into a homogeneous field of understanding, seen from the final point of view? Either choice would have the effect of privileging one term over another by the very form/process of the book. The reader can skip to the Introduction's concluding remarks to see how this is confronted (avoided).

No doubt there are other queries to the method and its theoretical underpinning (just another visual metaphor?). But is not all theory in any case a necessary fiction that can only be disproved and never in any final sense proved? 'In the current postmodern climate' (itself an assumption to be qualified in the chapter on postmodernism and history) it seemed and still seems the best way forward. Part II challenges the framework that theory propagates for itself and as such serves to contexualise not just theory but also the material and arguments of Part I.

The initial starting-point, as already stated, is the desire to mediate between sociohistorical methodologies/theories and those theories and methodologies based upon *a priori* assumptions of textual autonomy and immanence. In itself, the idea is not new. As it stands and is understandable today it probably goes back to the initial tensions in Formalism, tensions between hermeneutics and poetics, synchrony and diachrony. A mediation has been suggested by, most importantly, Jerome J. McGann in *Social Values and Poetic Acts: The Historical Judgment of Literary Work*,[22] and Hans Robert Jauss, the latter going so far as to suggest that it would involve a paradigm shift after the nature of Kuhn's scientific revolutions. This shift would require the following:

1. The mediation of aesthetic/formal and historical/reception-related analysis, as well as art, history, and social reality;
2. The linking of structural and hermeneutical methods (which hardly take note of their respective procedures and results);
3. The probing of an aesthetics (no longer related solely to description) of effect [*Wirkung*] and a new rhetoric which can equally well account for 'high-class' literature as well as popular literature and phenomena of the mass media.[23]

This is indeed how an attempt at mediation might have proceeded. But it is certainly easier to state the programme than to carry it out in this way since it takes too much on trust the nature of Literature, even as it realises some of the attendant problems. The tangential approach adopted by the book is an attempt to deal with this. However, it may still seem like a foolish hope to reconcile theories that on the one hand claim that texts are self-sufficient (even in their auto-deconstruction) and on the other hand theories that begin with the premise that text and context are inseparable. The argument thus delineated can be reduced to the confrontation between two diametrically opposed beliefs/theories (the distinction between belief and theory dependent upon whether one can argue from *a priori* grounds or not). What is the answer? *Is* there an answer? Is the task unrealistic? Have I constructed the problem in such a way that precludes not only an answer but the question itself? But this returns us to objections already considered.

The perspectives taken are from the point of view of 'the author', 'intention', 'postmodernism and history', and 'value'. Overlap, or 'imbrication', is inevitable since we are looking in each chapter at the same object, and the mediation is a way of tackling the cohabitative existence in the study of Literature of mutually incompatible theories. It could be said that this cohabitation illustrates that in one sense the problematic starting-point of the book is already in a state of liberal resolution. But the solution of allowing both immanence-based and sociohistorical-based theories to exist side-by-side in their various self-validating, functionally autonomous forms is fundamentally a 'liberal' solution, and presupposes a theoretical base of 'liberalism' or 'pluralism', that is, it is not an innocent solution. The liberal argument would have it that both sociohistorical and immanent approaches/theories are capable of yielding worthwhile/valid/rich/interesting interpretations and are not necessarily mutually exclusive at the practical level of reading, although they remain incompatible at the theoretical level. In this solution, therefore, poststructuralist and sociohistorical methods are being used as specific tools within the broader (practical) framework of 'reading', 'interpretation' without regard to the ideological theories supporting those tools. This is perhaps the state of affairs at present in higher education where a range of literary theories is taught without the expectation that students should discriminate between them in terms of value, or even necessarily to apply any theory with rigour. Or, as Steven Connor puts it in *Postmodernist Culture*:

> Far from being the theoretical monolith that it has been represented as since the 1970s, the universe of English studies has actively fostered subuniverses of different approaches and practices, in frictionless rapprochement.[24]

Theories have (theory has) been appropriated (or never escaped) the broader framework of a liberal-humanist education system. In this state of affairs theory is, ultimately, irrelevant, and we are left, in terms of the broad structure, with the pre-New Critical approach. This plurality of approaches might also be called the 'postmodern' solution – that is, if postmodernism can be said to 'prescribe' as well as to describe – since (neo)pragmatism and pluralism appear to be integral to definitions of postmodernism. Yet it it can hardly be an acceptable solution for those engaged in theoretical endeavour.

One of the most clear-sighted appraisals of the situation is Ian Small and Josephine Guy's essay 'English in Crisis (2)'. It is worth quoting their conclusion in full since it proposes a well-defined way forward:

> A precondition for resolving these disputes has to be an agreement about what theory is to explain, for theories can only be tested (and then rejected or accepted) when there is a prior agreement about what they are to do. It is only when the issue of defining the object of study in English is resolved through the establishment of a general agreement as to what it is, that questions about the adequacy of the theories used – their coherence, their utility, and their relationship to practice – may be addressed.[25]

Yet the problem remains that their programme is grounded by pragmatism, no doubt pedagogical, and utilitarianism. In fact, it would be quite easy to resolve the situation on these grounds, and for pedagogical purposes this may even be the way forward. But the book takes the stand that Literature, as previously stated, is more than its relation to pedagogy and criticism, and rather than take Small and Guy's suggestion suspends in Part I a definition of Literature and attempts to work inductively through a variety of categories, (although it does briefly address the issue in terms of Literature as an 'object' again at the end of Chapter 2). It looks at 'the author', 'intention', 'history' and 'value', and shows that the attacks upon these traditional areas by most (if not all) theory since the New Critics has failed to displace them, both logically and empirically. Part II is more categorical in how it defines and views Literature, and claims to have consequences for pedagogy, but probably not in the way Small and Guy perceived a solution.

Besides the liberal cohabitation solution, there is another solution which might also be claimed to be in existence, either as a result of practical exigencies, or because Literature is farther than ever from a definition of what constitutes it. This solution might be classed as that where the approach is of a specific political nature, Marxism or feminism for example. Here, theory and practice remain subordinate to the overriding political ends, they are subsumed within the 'action' of Marxism or feminism and need only conform to these political agendas; the particular political agenda remains the final arbiter. It could be argued that liberal-humanism is also of a specific political nature with its own agenda. However, it is as well to distinguish between what is dominant (hegemonical), and what is operating within (or tolerated though in opposition to) that ideology. The problem of cohabiting incommensurate systems remains as above, although it may be the case that because Marxism and feminism operate within the sphere of liberal-humanism different criticisms and analyses should be applied.

Part II, as it has been hinted at throughout the preceding remarks, is in stark contrast to Part I. The theme that runs through Part I of the book, but which was certainly not envisaged at the outset, is the question that has already occurred time and again in this introduction: What is Literature? No doubt this was short-sightedness on my part, but having started with a desire to mediate between immanence-based theories and sociohistorically-based theories, the best way forward appeared to be to look at this specific proposition from a number of angles that suggested possible resolutions or mediations – a procedure which at each turn necessitated a confrontation with the problem of just what constituted Literature. It has occurred, either through theoretical rigour or through some procedural flaw on my part, that to attempt mediation is inextricably bound up with how Literature is construed in the first place. I have already suggested that whatever the case is, we can observe something that is designated as Literature. Each angle at which the object is approached brings its own set of presumptions about what constitutes the object under investigation. If, for example, I believe a text is autonomous, intrinsically literary, what constitutes Literature for me will be a consequence of that (and vice versa). If I tend to see 'literary works' as a kind of writing that has no intrinsic 'literariness', the consequence may well be that I view Literature as an elitist construction that is part of the ideological state apparatus. No number of different angles can alter this problem, since, as already stated, I do not have a statue before me. But rather than explicate the shift here, the reader can either regard the book as 'process' and wait till Part II to discover just exactly what the shift involves, or may regard the book as 'structure' and simply read the introduction to that part as a continuation of this one.

Part I

2
Making the Author Function: The Wives of Thomas Pynchon and Paul de Man

How is it possible to defeat not the authors but the functions of the author, the idea that behind each book there is someone who guarantees a truth in that world of ghosts and inventions by the mere fact of having invested in it his own truth, of having identified himself with that construction of words?[1]

The aim of this chapter is to explore the possibility of mediation between the two camps by examining the notion of the author. The promise here is that a mediation might be achieved if some concept of the author can be brought back into those areas of literary theory which base themselves solely on notions of 'the text' and/or the primacy of language as a self-sufficient structure, areas which I term immanence-oriented or immanence-based theories, since meaning (and deferral of meaning) are believed to be immanent in the text. Since New Criticism, and perhaps especially since the Barthes essay 'The Death of the Author',[2] the author and everything associated with that term has been dismissed in most theory (the quotation from Calvino's postmodern novel shows that the death of the author is no stranger to fiction either). The author in all capacities has been mostly disregarded as a source of meaning and authority, and with it the Romantic legacy of the individual writer who is inspiring and inspired. Even for someone like E. D. Hirsch who proposes the necessity of author intentions, the author is simply the site of interpretative decidability and no more.[3] Paul de Man puts it as bluntly as this: 'Considerations of the actual and historical existence of writers are a waste of time from a critical viewpoint.'[4] Antagonism to the notion of the author remains very strong. Even extrinsic criticisms seem reluctant to look at the author, and are more likely to concentrate on the social and historical contexts. This is not to say that interest in the author has disappeared; biographies remain very popular, as Barthes notes in his essay, and biographical detail is often casually introduced into discussion of texts, even if just for anecdotal interest, it being understood that the information carries no theoretical weight. In the present theoretical domain, it is as if Barthes and de Man have been taken at their word.

Because the first aim of the book is to mediate between immanence-oriented theories and methodologies and sociohistorical theories and methodologies, the approach in this chapter is to concentrate on text-based theory, since this is where the argument is most hostile to the concept of the author and needs to be at its most persuasive. It therefore ignores arguments from the other camp which already incorporate 'the author', such as Hirsch and some feminist theories. I shall begin with the Barthes essay 'The Death of the Author', at the forefront of structuralist and poststructuralist attacks on the author, and exemplary in that it contains the major objections to the notion of the author. Also, the essay itself provides us with the possibility that if we can re-incorporate the author in some way into formalist/structuralist/poststructuralist theories, mediation becomes automatic between these and sociohistorical theories and methodologies if we follow the logic of the essay. This is because Barthes's essay suggests that the concept of the author is interrelated to 'society, history, psyche and liberty'. For Barthes, to remove the author, which is what he strives for, would be to remove these other elements. So if we can recuperate the author, whilst taking into account those arguments that removed the author in the first place, then society and history can be reintroduced on a formal level, and not just the methodological. There is also some sense of urgency to this project due to what has become known as the case of Paul de Man (and more recently Philip Larkin).

What has been put at stake, according to some critics, is the whole field of poststructuralism, a discursive regime which has eschewed notions of authors and origins in favour of texts and textuality, a doctrine which now appears to some to have enormous implications in the light of the revelations that during the Second World War Paul de Man wrote for a collaborationist journal in Belgium, and that he never chose to disclose that fact during his academic career in America. It sharply illustrates the problems immanence-based theories have, not just in the theoretical realm, but in the relationship between theory and ethics. The issue has forced critics to draw up battle-lines. On the one side numerous allies of deconstruction have leaped to de Man's defence, theorists and critics such as Geoffrey Hartmann, Jonathan Culler, J. Hillis Miller and Jacques Derrida. On the other side one critic has extrapolated from the revelation of de Man's early collaborationist writings to declare that there were 'grounds for viewing the whole of deconstruction as a vast amnesty project for the politics of collaboration during World War II'.[5] There is clearly much riding on the standing of 'the author' within theory. The de Man case illustrates that the question of an author's impingement upon the text is very much alive.[6] The obvious embarrassment caused to the defenders of deconstruction and de Man is surely evidence that all is not well in immanence-based theory – that authors and texts are linked in ways which affect our readings, our understanding, interpretation and the possible generation of meaning. If it were not the case, there would be no problem – the texts bearing the name 'de Man' would remain unaffected by any knowledge of his biographical details, or, to apply what Paul de Man himself wrote, any considerations of the actual and historical existence of the writer Paul de Man would be a waste of time when discussing the theoretical venture with which his name is associated (structuralism and poststructuralism). Are these questions ethical ones that have no place in immanence-orientated literary theories, or theory of any kind, or do we need once again to re-incorporate the author in some way?

Looking closely at the Barthes essay it soon becomes clear that the argument is based upon a number of unsubstantiated premises and internal contradictions. He begins the essay with a sentence from a Balzac short story and then asks the question 'Who is speaking thus?'. He goes through a series of related questions, all of which suggest answers to the overriding question, and all of which he dismisses. 'We shall never know', he concludes, 'for the good reason that writing is the destruction of every voice, of every point of origin'.[7] He naturalises the unsubstantiated premise – writing is the destruction of every voice, of every point of origin – with the introduction of the phrase 'for the good reason that'. The rhetorical gesture gives the impression of an *a priori* grounding for the death of the author. Yet it is apparent that at this point in his essay Barthes presents us with a question of faith, no more, no less. Barthes makes an equally dubious *a priori* statement upon which to build his argument when he asserts that writing is a neutral space without a voice. But it later transpires that this voicelessness is not at all intrinsic to writing. 'The removal of the Author ... is not merely an historical fact or an act of writing; it utterly transforms the modern text ....'[8] This is where Barthes visibly falters. The first part of the sentence incorporates two mutually exclusive ideas: that the removal of the author is on the one hand intrinsic to the act of writing, yet, on the other, contingent upon modern forces and knowledge. Now, if the removal of the author is an historical event, it is contingent and there is nothing to stop its re-introduction at some stage in the future (for instance, *now*, right this minute). But if it *is* intrinsic to the act of writing then it is ahistorical, not contingent at all, writing *is* always that neutral space without a voice, nothing to do with history, the author's demise always is (always was) coincidental with the written word. Yet Barthes here uses what amounts to an historical argument, since it is only recently, according to him, that linguistics has shown how this destruction of the author can be achieved. What linguistics has shown, then and now, must be a moot point, since linguistics itself, just like literary studies, remains divided as to what its object of study is – is it language as an autonomous structure, or is it language as it functions in society and from which it cannot be regarded separately (Saussure versus Voloshinov)? The paradox of the first half of Barthes's proposal creates problems for the second. To which element does the second part of the Barthes sentence, 'it utterly transforms the modern text', relate to? Does it relate to an historical fact, or does it relate to a function of language as proposed by a certain group of linguists, itself highly debatable? The second half of the statement is proposing the notion that modern writers and modern linguistics do not believe in the author, and this leads to the existence of our modern texts. It is not that there is some unassailable logic at work here, with the apprehension that writing is a process that of necessity precludes notions of the author; Barthes's argument is entirely historical, saying that we have entered a new era.

This point is emphasised a little further on where he continues to promote with broad historical generalisations what he considers to be *a priori*. 'The fact is', he writes, and then in parentheses, '(or, it follows) that *writing* can no longer designate an operation of recording, notation, representation, "depiction".'[9] Exactly what is being said here? Is it that writing has lost its previous function due to historical circumstances? Or is he saying that it logically follows that it *cannot* have that function, in which case it never has? The essay yearns for a logical argument derived from first principles, whilst its real base is a historical one. As such, its argument depends upon whichever history of writing and linguistics is chosen from the variety of possible narratives of writing available. This will decide whether we are to believe that the author is dead or not. There is no *a priori* reason for choosing one path over another, unless the theorist is prepared to accept at face value Barthes's potted history of writing from time immemorial to the 1960s.

If we stop at this point in the Barthes essay to view it within its own terms of reference there are a number of things that can be said. Historically speaking the necessity for the author has never been as consistently important as the essay makes out. The removal of the author *by* the author from the text is not a phenomenon of modern times. Neither Daniel Defoe's *Roxana* or Samuel Richardson's *Pamela* appeared in the first instance as being 'authored' in the Barthesian sense, best understood as a version of the 'auteur' in film theory. In Shakespearean times copyright was with the company putting the play on and not with the ostensible author (auteur). Works have appeared and been promoted as 'voiceless', to use Barthes's notion. Historically speaking, Barthes's argument is a non-starter. Similarly, we might choose a different linguistic model as having the historical ascendancy, a socio-linguistic model for instance that presents a communication paradigm of sender–message–receiver. In this case it would be *necessary* to take the author into account.

Another starting point in the Barthes essay might be derived from answering the question 'Who speaks thus?'. Barthes's suggestions are that it could be the hero of the story, Balzac the individual, Balzac the author, universal wisdom, Romantic psychology. Barthes's reasoning is that if it is not one of these voices, it cannot be decided, for writing is where all identity is lost. Yet could we not say that it is all of these voices? After all, three pages later Barthes is asserting that the text is where 'a variety of writings, none of them original, blend and clash'.[10] When put like this the text is being conceptualised in Bakhtinian terms, 'heteroglossia', a clashing of various languages. When put like this Barthes is also implying that the text is a site of contexts whose many interactions create meanings that cannot be controlled in any way except by the unification each reader produces or creates, an idea that has obvious parallels with de Man's hermeneutic circles (see next chapter). 'Who is speaking thus?' Barthes asks. Although the question may be pertinent, the answer he gives is inapplicable. One reason for that must be that he poses it in terms of speech and replies in terms of writing. His initial question is really 'Who is *writing* thus?'. And to follow his (whose?) argument, there are many writers, that is, many contexts. However, taken like this, the text begins to dissolve or disappear into those various contextual authorings Barthes has already dismissed (society, history, psyche), a criticism often levelled at extrinsic approaches.

How is it possible to take note of the fact that contexts are inscribed within texts and get no more out of the text than the contexts the reader is willing to appropriate? In fact, this is what the Barthes essay proposes, that it is only possible to disentangle texts, there can be no deciphering and hence no discovery of some ultimate secret meaning. Yet Barthes's description is based on an assumption that a text is the sum of these discrete parts, and no more. This is not the case. Criticising the Barthes essay at this juncture might proceed along the following lines. The only power the author has, according to his (?) essay, is the ability to mix writings. Barthes writes here in such a way as to demean this ability, and the reason this power is demeaned is because of what has already been said – namely that texts, according to Barthes, are no more than a clash of various writings, *none of which are original*. If we relate it back to the Balzac excerpt, the Barthesian answer to the question 'Who speaks thus?' should really be that it is an admixture of all the possible voices suggested. (This is a contradiction in the essay, for Barthes says we shall never know who speaks thus, and yet he 'disentangles' the text to provide precisely those voices – or clashes of writing.) If we take this one step further, and address the issue of *one voice*, that is, the author, it follows that the author is the person who has the power to create this juxtaposition/admixture/entanglement of writings. This specific concatenation of the different writings that go to make up a text is *unique*. There is no sense of inevitability in what Barthes writes here, that the particular entanglement of writings constituting the Balzac short story were destined to shuffle together in the way they do. What the essay is in fact presenting us with, although it tries to deride it, is the very author function it is seeking to eradicate.

This would amount to very little, perhaps, if it were not for the fact that this admixture of writing is both unique *and* cannot be a mere summation of discrete parts. It is arguable in the first instance whether the text *is* an admixture rather than something more hopelessly enmeshed beyond recognition and disentanglement. The writings do not function discretely but impinge upon one another to generate something other than a simple summation of the elements. This is the power of the author function in Barthesian terms, elide it though the essay tries. Certainly Barthes's spatial metaphor would be correct if each writing were discrete, distinct, and open to disentanglement from the other writings with which it inhabits and shares the text. But this is not certain (and perhaps where 'writings' are easily disentangled it is thought of as 'poor' Literature). Even if we were to adhere to Barthes's spatial metaphor it would still fail because 'the secret meaning' that Barthes says does not exist *under* the writings, it exists at the point where the writings clash, in the interstices of the writings. This ability to generate these unique juxtapositions is the originality of the author, and it is at the same time how we recognise the author's voice, not beneath, but at the boundaries or intersections of the various entanglements. The notion of author as an original creator with a unique voice cannot be discarded, it is a fact of the text that has its direct correlative with the actual historical existence of the author.

Now it might be argued that simply to reclaim the uniqueness of the creating author does not answer the objection that the author's relation to the text has nothing to do with the interpretation of the text. This objection can be categorised into three main areas. Firstly is the notion of the author as god, the place where all meaning is said finally to reside. Objections here often take the form that it implies a phallogocentric way of looking at the world, or that in a postmodern age the very concept of final and irrefutable truths is untenable. Secondly there is the objection of intention, which broadly speaking argues that it can never be known what authors have in mind when they write, and so it is useless for critics to attempt to work their way back from the text to an author's intentions, or vice versa, in an attempt to fix meaning or meanings. The third type of objection is related to formalist approaches and poststructuralist views on language which will only consider to be theoretically valid work done on the text itself, and will therefore disallow extrinsic commentary and knowledge, unless perhaps it is perceived as textually based. The recuperation of the author, and any attempt to make the author function again, has to take into account all three objections. I will discuss only the first objection here. The argument related to intention is examined in the next chapter. The third objection is the immanent-based theoretical argument already under general discussion as part of the two-camp scenario.

The objection to the author as god – the source and final arbiter of all meaning (and anything else we care to mention) – is a mixture of a number of dismissals that we can disentangle to reveal that none of them has any theoretical validity. We have already seen and discounted as theoretically inept the objection deriving from a distaste for the Romantic concept of the author as inspired genius. A further dismissal is founded upon a belief that it is reprehensible to place meaning in a framework that aligns itself with a notion of male authority. This is also essentially a moral argument and not a theoretical objection. Claims to a theoretical rationale do not hold up, as argued most persuasively by Patrick Colm Hogan in his chapter on feminist theory in *The Politics of Interpretation: Ideology, Professionalism, and the Study of*

Literature.[11] It can also be argued on moral grounds from the other side, that to deny any link between the writing and the author is to deny responsibility and culpability, a stance that has obvious consequences in the instance of Paul de Man's writings for *Le Soir*. The whole concept of phallogocentrism, as Hogan puts it, rests on the dubious metaphor of a penis having some equivalence with a quest for unity, totality and monologism, and hence totalitarianism and repression.

The third and final dismissal we can disentangle is the Derridean argument that attacks the Western metaphysical traditional presumption that meaning is fully present (in itself, to itself, for us). The argument here is that to look to the author as the authority for meaning rests on the desire and belief that presence guarantees truth in some way, as in speech-situations where the presence of the speaker is taken as a guarantee for what is being said. To seek 'the author' is to seek this presence. It is also to subscribe to a belief that words and meaning can be fully present to one another. However, this is the absolutist line of poststructuralist and deconstructionist thinking that really sets up a straw target: that some people (critics, theoreticians, readers, authors) hold an absolute belief in the transparency of language and its ability to give unmediated access to reality, and concomitantly complete access through writing to the author and his/her meaning. Once again I refer the reader to the comments in the introduction that subscription to absolutes is not part of the current theoretical agenda. The reader might also refer to Raymond Tallis's *Not Saussure*[12] and chapter 2 of Hogan's *The Politics of Interpretation*.[13]

At about the same time as Barthes, Michel Foucault too addressed the status of the author in 'What Is an Author?' (1969).[14] In this he notes four characteristics of what he terms 'the author function'. If we now look at these in addition to the Barthes analysis we will have broached a fairly comprehensive critique of 'the author'.

Firstly Foucault claims that 'discourses are objects of appropriation' and that 'Texts, books, and discourses really began to have authors ... to the extent that authors became subject to punishment.'[15] Thus, 'the author function is linked to the juridicial and institutional system that encompasses, determines, and articulates the universe of discourses'.[16] This remains the case of course, but how much attention should we pay to it in the realm of theory and criticism? The juridicial system (presumably Foucault means in terms of copyright) does appear to have some bearing upon the issue, but the cases of Larkin and de Man surely indicate that the author's impingement has nothing to do with their legal status, but rather with their social lives. What of the institutional system? It is not clear what Foucault means in this instance. This first characteristic of the author function is probably the least important in the form that Foucault traces it, since it is placed purely in historical terms and not in any theoretical nexus. We might note that a third link besides the juridicial and institutional ones is perhaps an ethical one, as already hinted at above, where the author becomes subject to moral censure. However, in the fourth characteristic of the author function, Foucault makes a distinction between 'the writer' and 'the author'. In the case of Paul de Man this would mean that our moral judgement, whichever way that went, would be upon 'the writer' with an 'actual and historical existence' and not upon 'the author', which is a construct in reading. This distinction is dealt with a little later on.

The second characteristic, like the first, is a historical comment: 'The author function does not affect all discourses in a universal and constant way.'[17] For example, Middle Age scientific discourse had 'authors' which guaranteed the 'true' by virtue of their name, whereas anonymous texts such as epics and tragedies gained their status from their ancientness.[18] We might take this as a word of caution on Foucault's part, and align it with Barthes in the sense that it shows that the notion of the author function is historically contingent (for Barthes the modern period has witnessed the author's necessary demise). Characteristics one and two as described by Foucault illustrate that the author function is a construct and not a theoretical given.

This is a point made most forcefully in the third characteristic, which is that the author function 'does not develop spontaneously as the attribution of a discourse to an individual. It is, rather, the result of a complex operation which constructs a certain rational being that we call "author"'. Foucault claims that:

these aspects of an individual which we designate as making him an author are only a projection, in more or less psychologizing terms, of the operation that we force texts to undergo, the connections that we make, the traits that we establish as pertinent, the continuities that we recognise, or the exclusions that we practice.[19]

Here we have the crux of the author function, and the reason, no doubt, why it is called a 'function' rather than simply 'the author' (although Foucault rather loosely interchanges the two). According to Foucault, we do not link a text to the author (more correctly 'the writer' in Foucauldian terms), which is presumably what we imagine we are doing when we talk about the author, but work on the text in a specific mode, placing it or them in a discursive mode called 'the author function'. We could say from this that 'the author function', when we choose to operate a text in this manner, is coterminous with the text itself. In other words, 'the author function' is not a 'context', a 'background' against which we can place a particular text or texts, it is a way of reading and making connections and explaining and interpreting. Foucault's objection to this runs along ethical lines, much as we found Barthes's real objections came down to moral preferences rather than objections along any *a priori* theoretical grounds. Foucault sees the author's ideological function not as the traditional place where 'meaning begins to proliferate, to proliferate indefinitely', as a source of genius etc., but as allowing 'a limitation' of the proliferation of meaning.[20] We can sense Foucault's distaste for the author function when he states:

> the author does not precede the works; he is a certain functional principle by which, in our culture, one limits, excludes, and chooses; in short, by which one impedes the free circulation, the free manipulation, the free composition, decomposition, and recomposition of fiction.[21]

Yet Foucault realises that to imagine or claim the possibility that fiction could 'operate in an absolutely free state' without any such constraint is 'pure romanticism', but still looks forward to a time when we do not ask the questions 'who spoke?', 'how deeply/authentically/originally?'. Foucault's express desire is to make us indifferent to the author function, so that we can claim, like Beckett, 'What difference does it make who is speaking?'[22] Instead Foucault wants to shift the emphasis of interest onto questions of power and discourse and their modes of existence. But in all this, as with Barthes, it should be noted that there are no *theoretical* objections to the notion of an author. Instead, they are founded on ideological and ethical grounds. And just as it was possible to turn the Barthes essay back on itself in arguing for the possibility of an 'original' 'voice' after all – whether we choose to accept it or not (an ethical or political choice, not a theoretical one) – we can likewise turn the Foucault article back on itself and state that the author function can be retrieved if we so desire since there is nothing theoretically anathema to it. The most useful aspects of Foucault's (whose? his? Foucault has decreed that there shall be no collected works of Foucault – free circulation?) essay are the distinction between 'the writer' and 'the author function', and the notion that (if we go on to extrapolate from Foucault's argument) that the author function is coterminous with the text, that the author function is an operation the text undergoes.

It might seem in all this that I have avoided two central issues in dealing with 'the author', hiding in effect behind Barthes and Foucault. One would be the common-sense notion of 'the author' being 'the writer', a point that Foucault gets round by claiming this notion is as much a fallacy as identifying the 'I' of a piece of fiction with 'the writer' of the fiction. But can 'the author function' really be something completely distinct from 'the writer'? Are not the two linked in some inextricable way? To pose it as Foucault has is to posit that 'the author function' is constructed from the texts bearing the name of the author and has no connection with the 'real writer'. But can this be true? Whilst reading texts under 'the author function' might be an activity that regards both function and text as coterminous, the construction of that author function has involved 'the writer'. A concept such as 'the author function', as portrayed by Foucault, even without the re-introduction of the 'originating' and 'original' author that was retrieved from Barthes, would seem to hold out a possibility of the mediation this book seeks, since 'the author function' would include material normally considered extraneous to the text whilst itself being generated by those same texts. 'The author function' could, for example, quite easily contain all those elements Barthes considered anterior – 'society, history, psyche and liberty' – and yet still be an immanence-based theory. The problem is that 'the writer'/'author (function)' distinction is not complete. We can look at the possibility of distinguishing between 'the writer' and the 'author function', and at the notion of 'the originating author', through what I consider boundary cases, that is, cases that will stretch all of these ideas. For an analysis of 'the author function' there are the instances of Paul de Man and Thomas Pynchon.

'Thomas Pynchon is famous for not being "Thomas Pynchon"': the writer refuses to play the role of the author. We know a few 'facts' about the historical existence of Thomas Pynchon, date-of-birth, education, employment, ancestry. His conspicuous absence has generated its own apocrypha, such as Jules Siegel's article in *Playboy* entitled 'Who is Thomas Pynchon ... and Why Did He Take Off with My Wife?' in which Siegel claims to have been a friend of Pynchon's, as well as claiming that Pynchon had an affair with his wife, Chrissie.[23] Amongst other things, Jules provides us with Chrissie's assessment of Thomas Pynchon as a lover. At the other end of the scale, Weisenberger's introduction to *A 'Gravity's Rainbow' Companion: Sources and Contexts for Pynchon's Novel* goes out of its way to respect Thomas Pynchon's privacy, and prints just the basic publicly-known facts.[24]

As to Paul de Man, a critic often considered one of the main instigators and proponents of deconstruction in American academia, his 'fall' is not just a result of the silence he maintained about his past, but that

> [t]he scandal had to do with words and with silence, with what de Man wrote in Belgium and what he didn't say in America. Perhaps it wasn't coincidental that de Man's practice dealt on an abstract plane with words and with silence – and that there had long been those who felt that de Man's theory had the effect of silencing language.[25]

Lehman goes on to say 'The belated discovery of his wartime journalism had the effect of requiring his students to reconsider his entire mature oeuvre in the light of the belated revelations.'[26]

With Thomas Pynchon and de Man it is clear that we have facts about the writer/author that can impinge upon their works' meanings. Thomas Pynchon's works are renowned for their championing of people on the margins, 'human waste', people who have slipped through 'official' society. Pynchon's act of reclusiveness appears as a re-enactment of this marginalisation. It might also be taken as an act of subversion, a counterforce, even a counter-conspiracy, actions that have affinities with *Gravity's Rainbow* and other of his works. With Paul de Man, it is not only noted that his personal silence correlates with his philosophical standpoint, but that his style of writing and his personality commanded 'the rhetoric of authority', which is at odds with the denial of an authorising author.[27] Paul de Man was also a bigamist, although, like Pynchon's 'running-off' with Jules Siegel's wife, this does not loom large in the hermeneutic stakes. It is easy to see how in both cases these authors' texts are placed in a discursive mode called the 'author function' with regards to some information (collaboration and silence; reclusiveness, 'outside-the-system'), but not with regards to other items of information that are known (the relationship of wives to Paul de Man and Thomas Pynchon, for instance). We might separate out these two areas into two discursive fields, one called 'biography' and the other 'the author function'. From this it is feasible to say that 'the author function' is a text-generated discursive field since it is wholly dependent upon perceived textual meanings. The fact that Pynchon had an affair with someone's wife does not enter this 'author function' field because it is not part of the text's meaning(s).

To conclude this chapter, it is clear that the two main attacks of Barthes and Foucault on the sociohistorical notion of 'the author', along with their poststructuralist successors, are fundamentally flawed within their own delimitations (and if we take Barthes's point that all the other sociohistorical material comes along with this term, then it is basically the whole attack on the contextualist theoretical camp that is flawed). From the point of view of 'the author function', it appears fair to say that the mediation between the two camps is always already there. The author function as described by Barthes and Foucault is, despite their wishes to the contrary, there in the form of 'uniqueness' and 'the writer', concerns that are extrinsic with respect to their own formulations of hermeneutic textual immanence yet necessary to the author function. Whether we regard these factors as in some way generated by the texts themselves, as with the argument proposed above that only *certain* biographical details are critically pertinent to the text (wives, evidently, are not, at least in the cases of Paul de Man and Thomas Pynchon) and therefore in concordance with 'immanent' methodologies, theories and approaches, or whether we call those factors sociohistorical from the start, providing a nexus wherein the text can be fitted, is apparently beside the point. 'The author function' exists at all levels here discussed and *is* therefore a mediation. We can say that it is a necessary condition for our understanding of Literature. However, it is not a sufficient condition, and problems for mediation like those of 'intention', the status of knowledge (and meaning) in postmodern theory or the postmodern age, and evaluation, remain (although following the logic through of our assessment of the immanent camp of thinking the problems presumably have already disappeared). These are the concerns of the remaining chapters of Part I.

3
'Murder Case Man's "Threat" to Shoot Teddy Bears': Intention in Literary Theory

A man accused of murder in a petrol station robbery once lined up teddy bears in his bedroom and threatened them with a gun, a jury at Winchester crown court was told yesterday.

Marlene Thomas, aged 18, said she and her former boyfriend Mohammed Nazir were living with his co-accused, Jamil Chowdhary, in a squat in Oxford.

Miss Thomas said she saw Mr Nazir, aged 21, with a 2-ft long gun in the bedroom. 'There were some teddy bears, which he put on the floor. He just started fooling around, running around with the gun, pointing it at the teddy bears and saying: "which one's first?"'[1]

This newspaper clipping provides us with a good example of the problems and possibilities of intention, along with its accomplices, meaning and evidence. The first intention, the threat to shoot teddy bears, appears to vouchsafe for a second intention yet to be decided: the intent to murder. The fact that the accused threatened to kill teddy bears also suggests an unbalanced mind – the mind of a murderer (or the kind of mind that can contain the desire to murder). But why are there protective marks around the word 'threat'? Does this indicate the article's own doubts as to the validity of either interpretation of the facts, of the intention? Does the article, by inferring that a threat to shoot teddy bears is not a real threat, intend to undermine the connection that the prosecution makes between the two intentions? And what about me, the reader of the news? I find the article humorous, but am troubled because it appears on page 2 of a so-called respectable newspaper, traditionally a serious news page dealing with serious events, although not averse to comic ideas. I imagine other people will not find it funny at all, and might even find my use of it tasteless.[2] Is the intention to make me laugh? To make me laugh and think? And could that issue be decided if I asked the writer? And if he or she told me that it was intended to be a serious piece of journalism, what then happens to my response of laughter? Should I change it in the light of this evidence, or does it not matter? And then, what of the suspect? Did he really intend to kill the teddy bears? Would I be able to remove the protective marks from around the word 'threat' if the defendant, rather than the journalist, said it was the real intention? Why did he ask which teddy bear was first? Was *that* of any significance? Was it a rhetorical gesture, or did he really believe he was going to shoot the teddy bears and wanted to give them a choice? And was the intention of the journalist behind selecting this piece of information from the court proceedings for the article to show that the defendant was always, or at least potentially always, unstable? In all these areas, is the intention fundamentally related to the meaning in that if I find the intention I automatically have the meaning? And are these notions of intention and meaning the same when we talk about Literature, criticism and literary theory?

> I can know what your utterance means 'in itself'; what you intended your utterance to mean; what you mean by uttering it; what it 'really means'; what its words mean; and so on. And I can have a sense of knowing only a part of your meaning – what your words mean but not what you mean by them; what you mean to say but not what your words mean; the words but not (as we say) the tune.[3]

It is easy to understand from all these questions and problems why the idea of intention seems like the pot of gold at the end of the hermeneutic rainbow. Put simply, we would say that the meaning of a text is dependent upon what has been intended by the author. All interpretative difficulties, including questions of aesthetics, would be resolved by an appeal to whichever meaning or aesthetic strategy had been intended. We would then always be sure what a particular work of Literature meant by determining what the intentions had been. Other meanings attributed by readers could be discarded or classed as purely subjective. For all those concerned with the interpretation of Literature, (and this is everybody involved in the study of Literature – to say that Literature should just 'be' rather than 'mean' is really another interpretation – a point I shall return to in the second part), this methodological procedure might have the odd problem in practice, but at least the theory behind it would be clear and precise. An interpretation that proposed a meaning that could not be supported by evidence that showed the meaning was intended would be interesting, but could be rendered invalid. Literature might then approach some kind of scientific status, using information that could be brought forward as evidence to be judged in the court of literary criticism, much as the man who threatened the teddy bears was judged. My initial intention is to try to find the pot of gold.

At present, the weight of evidence against intention in literary theory very nearly amounts to a mathematical proof as to why, exactly, 'intention' is nothing more than 'fool's gold'. Just to be asked to even think about intention seems to be a request to trundle out arguments that have the air of redundancy. The very lack of current debate about it in literary academia would suggest that it has become an obsolete concept, despite the work of the odd hardened 'intentionalist' such as E. D. Hirsch, the kind of person who will just not listen to reason and revise his views. So whatever *did* happen to 'intention'? A review of its history should allow us to shed some light on the problems and possibilities.

Wimsatt and Beardsley

In Summer 1946 *The Sewanee Review* published an article by Wimsatt and Beardsley called 'The Intentional Fallacy'. It comes to us these days as the first essay in that New Critical classic *The Verbal Icon*.[4] Wimsatt and Beardsley place themselves and their article against a historical background where the notion that the author's intention is primary is already taken for granted. They are referring to that age we, like them, regard as prehistoric, a time when literary theory and criticism were populated by beliefs in, as Wimsatt and Beardsley put it: 'inspiration, authenticity, biography, literary history and scholarship'.[5] They succinctly describe the 'intentional fallacy' in another article as 'a confusion between the poem and its origins .... It begins by trying to derive the standard of criticism from the psychological *causes* of the poem and ends in biography and relativism'.[6]

There are two major issues with which the essay 'The Intentional Fallacy' is concerned. The first is to find a means of assessing the *worth* of a piece of literature, an idea that appears to have little validity in current literary theory. Nevertheless, it is worth noting that this is the context in which intention first appears since it demonstrates just how embedded and interlinked each of the issues in Part I have been in the past, and, so this Part shows, still are. Wimsatt and Beardsley's argument is 'that the design or intention of the author is neither available nor desirable as a standard for judging the success of a work of literary art ... '.[7] Here they are reacting against the belief that, as they say, 'In order to judge the poet's performance, we must know *what he intended.*'[8] The second issue is concerned with how we are to understand what a poem is about, although we take their arguments to hold good for Literature as a whole and not just poetry.

Their objections to intention are three-fold. Firstly, they argue that just because some designing intellect has caused the poem to come into existence this does not in any way grant a standard from which the work can be judged. The second and third reasons for dismissing intention are a mixture of New Critical dogma and psychology. I quote this in full because it underlies much of the subsequent thinking in the history of intention:

> One must ask how a critic expects to get an answer to the question about intention. How is he to find out what the poet tried to do? If the poet succeeded in doing it, then the poem itself shows what he was trying to do. And if the poet did not succeed, then the poem is not adequate evidence, and the critic must go outside the poem – for evidence of an intention that did not become effective in the poem.[9]

This first issue, that of evaluation, has no direct bearing on the second issue they tackle: the meaning of a work. It is, nevertheless, curiously linked, as the above comments would logically suggest, to the history of intention in that it becomes entangled in the question of interpretation, as we shall see later when we come to E. D. Hirsch. This second issue of meaning is ascribed much less emphasis in the essay. As with the 'Murder Case Man's "Threat" to Shoot Teddy Bears' text, it is a question of evidence. Wimsatt and Beardsley see 'a difference between internal and external evidence for the meaning of a poem'.[10] Today we would understand it as the difference between meaning as determined by considerations of the text itself, and meaning as determined by information gleaned from sources other than the text, in other words, the very antithetical camps we are attempting to mediate between. It seems that underlying their manoeuvre is the following problem: they first of all deny that what the author had intended to write can be any guide for judging the standard of a literary work's success. But having thrown author's intentions out for one reason they then use this very jettisoning as the basis for something essentially unconnected, the denial of the possibility that author's intentions can be used for authorising and determining meaning, which is entirely a separate issue. The problem is further compounded because they refuse to state categorically that once the author is removed meaning thus becomes immanent in the text. That is, they do not promote the notion that the meaning of a text is immanent in the text. This must beg the question 'Where does meaning reside?'.

Wimsatt and Beardsley do, in fact, provide answers to the issues of literary worth and meaning, and it is exactly the answer that the history of intention constantly provides us with in one form or another. They show us how we can judge a piece of work and how we can locate its meaning. For both judgement and meaning lie not with the author and his or her ephemera, and not, as we might have expected, with the autonomous text, but with what they call the public, what might be termed in today's jargon the social sphere. Having got rid of the author and the author's intention, they move on to concentrate on what kind of evidence can be used in the court of literary theory to support the semantic autonomy of the text. They divide this evidence into three types:

external, internal and the intermediate. Internal evidence, which is the text itself and is superficially regarded as private, is, they argue, already public, because language is in all instances social. External evidence, such as letters, journals, reported conversations, what is usually regarded as public, is really private, for, as they claim, it is 'not a part of the work as a linguistic fact'.[11] Their intermediate third type is 'about the character of the author or about private or semiprivate meanings attached to words or topics by an author or by a coterie of which he is a member'.[12] 'The difficulty for criticism', according to Wimsatt and Beardsley, is that all three types of evidence shade into each other. We could therefore summarise their argument and the difficulties entailed in the following manner: we cannot know what the author intended with regards to his or her work of art, for a mixture of psychological and epistemological reasons, as well as the New Critical status of the artefact, that is, as an autonomous and self-sufficient generator of meaning. Judgement of its success or failure as a work of art lies purely in the public domain. The meaning of the work also cannot be determined through recourse to author's intentions, since, as previously argued, these intentions are unknowable and irrelevant. Meanings, like evaluations, are social. We could describe Wimsatt and Beardsley's problem as a desire to regard the artefact as autonomous whilst simultaneously maintaining that the evaluations of it and meanings pertaining to it are in fact a function of social determinations. Right at the beginning of the history of intention we have the main characters and fault lines that can generate the rest of the narrative: the pull between language as self-sufficient and language as social, between our desire to find our evidence in the text and our desire to find it socially determined. I use the word desire. I could also use the word belief, since none of Wimsatt and Beardsley's arguments have *a priori* grounds. I want to hold to this tension between the social and the textual as the narrative thread that helps generate the history of intention.

We now move from 1942 to 1967, the first of two fifteen-year cycles in this history, when two notable events take place. The first event is the publication of E. D. Hirsch's *Validity in Interpretation*, which provides a defence for the primacy of the author's intentions in deciding meaning(s).[13] That the second event occurs in 1967 is not so certain. If it does, it is a lecture given by Paul de Man entitled 'Form and Intent in the American New Criticism'. We have no hard evidence for its existence until the publication in 1971 of *Blindness and Insight*.[14] The Preface to this book suggests the paper was given in either 1966 or 1967. However, for the sake of history and the sake of neatness, let us assume that both Hirsch and de Man entered the narrative of intention in the same year.

E. D. Hirsch

Beginning with Hirsch, what his book has to say about intention can most easily be understood by what his aim is, captured in the title *Validity in Interpretation*. According to Hirsch, the only time it is possible to have a valid interpretation is when there is a determinable meaning open to rational dispute, and this meaning has to be located in the author, 'For if the meaning of a text is not the author's, then no interpretation can possibly correspond to *the* meaning of the text, since the text can have no determinate or determinable meaning'.[15] So, to 'save the ideal of validity [the theorist] has to save the author as well'.[16] Hirsch actually agrees with Wimsatt and Beardsley's 'intentional fallacy' in so far as it applies to evaluation and judgement. That is, to judge the artistic success of, for example, Hardy's *Tess of the D'Urbevilles* and Hardy's effectiveness in communicating whatever it was he wanted to communicate, a distinction has to be made between the author's intentions and the work itself, otherwise there would be nothing to evaluate. But for Hirsch this activity should be classified as criticism, and not interpretation, although in practice judgement and the search for meaning are often intertwined. Unlike evaluation and criticism, which are subjective, for Hirsch meaning can be determined and adjudicated objectively. He is careful to state that he does not believe in certain knowledge, but in probabilities – in other words, given all the evidence, what is probably true. Hence, he is talking of validity and not of verification. To arguments that a work's meaning changes over time, he distinguishes between meaning and significance. The meaning, which is recoverable from the author's intentions, is consistent and unchangeable. What in fact changes is the significance of the work, how it compares to other works, for instance, or what relevance it has, or whether it is now considered beautiful. For Hirsch, significance also belongs in the domain of criticism and subjectivity, whereas interpretation is not open to those vagaries. For Hirsch, interpretation can objectively decide upon the most probable meaning of a text, that is, the meaning intended by the author.

Like Wimsatt and Beardsley, Hirsch proves to be a mess of contradictions. For instance, he claims that we need to distinguish between what a text means, and what it means *for* someone.[17] Hirsch is obviously only interested in the former, what the text means in itself, an argument which clearly tends towards New Criticism and text-autonomy. His argument goes on to show how we can determine this meaning. From what he has said previously we would be forgiven for expecting this to be conditional upon the author. But it is really nothing of the kind. Verbal meaning depends upon being able to determine what implications of a text should be included or excluded, for meaning depends upon implications, and these can be determined by narrowing down the class of the text as far as possible, something dependent upon tradition, date, genre, and in part the author, by virtue of the fact of whatever else he or she has written. A quotation from Hirsch's book shows just how superficially he appears to be mutually incompatible with Wimsatt and Beardsley, but in fact reiterates those very tensions, desires and beliefs we previously found:

> authorial will is a formal requirement for determinacy. Of equal importance is the sharability of verbal meaning, and for this the necessary requirement is the existence of shared conventions. Verbal meaning is both a willed type and a shared type.[18]

Immediately noticeable is the contrast between 'sharability of verbal meaning' and 'willed type'. The willed type takes us back to the text itself, which presupposes a consciousness behind the text, but is of no more consequence than that. Now 'shared type' is a confusion of two different things. It means both that verbal meaning is by its very nature sharable, social and that the text fits into shared, that is, conventional, categories, a referral back to tradition, date and genre. All this amounts to the same problematic we found in Wimsatt and Beardsley: the issues of where the meaning resides; what evidence can be used to decide it; what status that evidence is given. Wimsatt and Beardsley try to make the text semantically autonomous, try to make meaning reside in the text, or if we use the word 'belief' instead of desire, believe that the text is semantically autonomous. But they are unable to make it self-sufficient, nor do they believe it. Hirsch likewise tries to make meaning determinable, and in direct contrast to Wimsatt and Beardsley, with recourse to the author's intentions. He fares no better and has to resort to the 'sharability' of verbal meaning. In other words, and like Wimsatt and Beardsley, he resorts to meaning as socially determined. By the way, what then happens to intent and the author's intentions is unclear. A final blast from Hirsch will show how confused his argument against his predecessors is, for he says that beneath 'the intentional fallacy' and the notion of 'semantic autonomy' is an assumption of 'public consensus' which if true would render Wimsatt and Beardsley's arguments plausible. But for Hirsch no such consensus ever exists, 'The public meaning of a text is nothing more or less than those meanings which the public happens to construe from the text', and in any case, there never is such a consensus.[19] But if no consensus exists for public meaning, just how is his notion of sharability to be taken? How is a sharable verbal meaning different from a public meaning? The history of intention once again throws us into the social realm.

Paul de Man

Paul de Man's essay, 'Form and Intent in the American New Criticism', is an attempt to mediate between form and intent, and as such, in the history of intention, might be regarded as one of the first deliberate attempts to overcome the difficulties of that tension I outlined at the beginning between the New Critical autonomous text and what appears for them to be the unfortunate intrinsic social nature of language and Literature, unfortunate because it negates all New Critical arguments.[20] De Man believes he is working at a time when the notion of the autonomous aesthetic object is under threat, from structuralism in France, and in America from 'sociological, political, and psychological considerations'.[21] Presumably de Man was unaware of the 'threat' from Hirsch! De Man says 'The kind of autonomy to be found in literary works is certainly far from self-evident; it has to be redefined ....'[22]

Intention in Literary Theory

'Form and Intent' is an essay that packs in a large number of ideas on the question of intention in a way that suggests logical progression from one to the next. Yet at each stage it can be seen that there is no logical follow-on. De Man uses two sets of images with which to portray his notion of intention. The first set establishes a distinction between 'intentional objects', such as chairs, and 'natural objects', such as stones. 'Natural objects' can be described without any reference to intention, an object like a stone simply exists. Of the intentional object de Man says, 'the most rigorous description of the perceptions of the object "chair" would remain meaningless if one does not organise them in function of the potential act that defines the object; namely, that it is destined to be sat on'.[23] An 'allusion to the *use* to which it is put' is thus integral to the conception of the significance of the chair. Having delineated what constitutes an 'intentional object' de Man goes on to argue for the re-introduction of a concept of 'intention', believing that its suppression by Wimsatt and Beardsley in their formulation of 'the intentional fallacy' renders the 'status of literary language ... similar to that of a natural object'. De Man argues that their dismissal of intention, and the subsequent dismissal of intention by others, has been based on a false notion of intention. I quote it in some detail to illustrate what perhaps still persists to this day as the common understanding of intention (a 'remarkably tenacious' understanding de Man calls it), as well as illustrating de Man's own conception of structural intentionality which continues to use the image of a chair. Initially he is taking issue with Wimsatt and Beardsley's characterisation of intention in *The Verbal Icon*:

> 'Intent' is seen, by analogy with a physical model, as a transfer of a psychic or mental content that exists in the mind of the poet to the mind of a reader, somewhat as one would pour wine from a jar into a glass. A certain content has to be transferred elsewhere, and the energy necessary to effect the transfer has to come from an outside source called intention. This is to ignore that the concept of intentionality is neither physical nor psychological in its nature, but structural, involving the activity of a subject regardless of its empirical concerns, except as far as they relate to the intentionality of the structure. The structural

intentionality determines the relationship between the components of the resulting object in all its parts, but the relationship of the particular state of mind of the person engaged in the act of structurization to the structured object is altogether contingent. The structure of the chair is determined in all its components by the fact that it is destined to be sat on, but the structure in no way depends on the state of mind of the carpenter who is in the process of assembling its parts. The case of the work of literature is of course more complex, yet here also, the intentionality of the act, far from threatening the unity of the poetic entity, more definitely establishes this unity.[24]

In contrast to the chair image, which also represents the hypostasis of the 'poetic act', de Man turns to Northrop Frye's notion of intention, which for de Man is closer to Wimsatt and Beardsley's 'poetic act' *before* they have suppressed 'intention'. Here de Man introduces his second image set, that of a hunter taking aim (it appears impossible to discuss intention without having to shoot something or someone). De Man says a distinction must be made between the hunter who takes aim at a rabbit, and the hunter who takes aim at an artificial target. In the former, the 'intention' lies outside the act itself, that is, the intention to eat or sell the rabbit. The latter, according to de Man, is the true image for 'the aesthetic entity', since when the hunter

> takes aim at an artificial target, his act has no other intention than aim-taking for its own sake and constitutes a perfectly closed and autonomous structure. The act reflects back upon itself and remains circumscribed within the range of its own intent.[25]

Taking together the two image sets de Man uses (the chair, a hunter taking aim) it can be seen that he is presenting two illustrations of the same thing, the 'aesthetic entity', the first as it stands in relation to the notion of it as an intentional object (chair), and the second as it stands in relation to a particular type of intention (a hunter taking aim at an artificial target). But are they compatible? The chair's intentionality is a function of its use. It is its intended use that organises its parts, that gives it its structure.

Intention in Literary Theory

But how are we to relate this to the hunter taking aim? If it is 'use' that is the significant element then the chair is surely akin to the hunter who kills the rabbit rather than the hunter who aims at an artificial target, since the 'use' is outside the act itself, just as the use of the chair is not circumscribed within its own limits. The 'intentionality' of the chair's structure can only be defined and described by resorting to what is outside. To put it another way, the chair is not 'aimed' at itself, autonomous, it requires a sitter. The image of intention as represented by the chair is therefore invalidated when it comes to its applicability in relation to de Man's discussion of the 'aesthetic object'.

But perhaps this reading is in bad faith. It is possible that 'the chair' is only used by de Man when he wants to present the idea of hypostasis in Wimsatt and Beardsley, and that the 'hunter' image is not a refinement of the previous ('founding') image, but used to represent the 'poetic act'. In which case we must now take the image of the hunter aiming at an artificial target as in some sense also representing an intentional object, with the status of a founding (grounding) image. But if we are to take this image seriously – and how can we not since it now forms the basis for the essay's understanding of intention? – the idea of intention as structuring all parts becomes problematic. We are no longer able to allude to 'use', in the way we could with the chair, as constituting any description of intention. There is no 'use', since de Man classes the aesthetic object as being of the same ontological status as that of a toy (although even here there would be problems since not all toys are ends in themselves, some are designed with educational purposes specifically in mind). If the hunter aiming at an artificial target 'has no other intention than aim-taking for its own sake', then an aesthetic object can surely have no other intention than the constitution of an aesthetic object for its own sake.[26] This is the conclusion that must be drawn if the analogy is to be followed through. Unity will be achieved since all parts will be organised according to the intention of the aesthetic object to be an aesthetic object. Obviously this is simply a variation of the 'art-for-art's-sake' argument, and as such a dead-end. However, the essay shifts its ground again in what is yet another non sequitur. It now begins to talk of 'meaning'.

For de Man, the 'deliberate rejection of the principle of intentionality' has led to a forgoing of a perception of '"the struggle with meaning" of which all criticism, including the criticism of forms, should give an account'.[27] But which image are we meant to take to help understand the struggle with 'meaning'? If the essay wishes to reclaim 'intent', how is 'meaning' meant to correlate with it? Is 'meaning' *separate* from 'intent'? De Man's implication is that if 'intent' can be re-introduced as a basic premise for any description of an aesthetic object, 'the struggle with meaning' automatically returns. Unfortunately, the essay leaves this possibility up in the air and moves from the theoretical realm to the practical outcome of New Criticism and Formalist criticism. De Man claims that the work of the New Critics, based on their belief in the 'organic' unity of the poetic text, was shattered by the very results of their analyses, namely, the discovery that through such features as irony and ambiguity texts have a plurality of meanings. It is tempting to ask that if this is the case then were they not engaged in 'the struggle with meaning' all the time? However, the essay argues that the unity always found in texts is not a feature of the texts themselves but of the reader involved in the hermeneutic process or circle. This must surely negate his attempt to redefine, through the concept of intentional structure, the aesthetic object as autonomous, since de Man's appeal to the reader now throws the object once more into the social realm, as we have seen so often throughout the history of intention. The explanation given is:

> because such patient and delicate attention was paid to the reading of forms, the critics pragmatically entered into the hermeneutic circle of interpretation, mistaking it for the organic circularity of natural processes.[28]

This reads as a very similar conclusion to Barthes's proclamation of the birth of the reader at the expense of the death of the author. De Man is asserting that the totality or unity which has constantly been achieved by critics resided in the reading process ('the act of interpreting the text')[29] and not in the texts themselves. This view takes the aesthetic object away from the idea of immanence that the chair image proffers. It begs the question of precisely how the chair image is to be understood.[30] Depending upon how the essay is now evaluated, de Man's argument is confused, confusing, elusive or illogical (or all). It takes two aspects from Heidegger's theory of hermeneutic circularity:

> The first [aspect] has to do with the epistemological nature of all interpretation. Contrary to what happens in the physical sciences, the interpretation of an intentional act or an intentional object always implies an *understanding* of the intent.[31]

A little further on he refines this:

> To interpret an intent, however, can only mean to understand it. No new set of relationships is added to an existing reality, but relationships *that were already there* are being disclosed, not only in themselves (like the events of nature) but as they exist for us.[32]

De Man delimits the hermeneutic circle to one that discovers the intention of the intentional/aesthetic object. There is no mention of 'meaning' now. If what I have said to this point holds true then de Man can only be saying that the interpretative (reading) process discovers the fact that the aesthetic object intends (aims toward) being an aesthetic object. What has happened to the 'struggle with meaning'? The problem remains that de Man does not make explicit the connection between 'intent' and 'meaning'. Whilst appearing to talk about the former, he suggests the latter, a suggestion that implies reading of the form (the aesthetic, autonomous structuring) can discover the structural intent and that this automatically leads to (or is) meaning. It is in effect a mediation between the two camps – but is achieved through a process of non sequiturs, and is not therefore logically sustainable. He says that the New Critics, in pushing their interpretative processes to the limit, discovered not one meaning but a plurality of significances (do significances = meanings at this juncture?). Is it the same thing when he says, 'Far from being something added to the text, the elucidating commentary simply tries to reach the text itself, whose full richness is there at the start.'[33] But 'full richness' in what sense? At this point in the essay the reader would logically conclude that it was the 'full richness' of intentions. Taking stock of de Man's essay this far we might say that a text could (1) only have a single intention which would organise all constituent parts (the intention of an aesthetic object, presumably immanent), and/or (2) be discovered to have unity as a result of entering the hermeneutic circle. To follow de Man's argument, we will have a plurality of hermeneutic circles, each discovering an intention ('meaning'?). We will have, in other words, a text that is plurally autonomous, in the sense that instead of *one* observable structurisation it has a number. The reader thus has the opportunity to catch hold of a different structure or aesthetic intentionality each time the hermeneutic circle is entered. These intentions must always be immanent in the text, otherwise it could only be understood as something completely foisted onto the text by the reader. Presumably, however, we must make the leap for ourselves that de Man never makes, and assume that it is 'meaning' that is equivalent to 'intention', since there is only one understanding of intention in the essay with respect to this. De Man's confusion lies in his conflation of poetics and hermeneutics, if we take poetics to be how the text functions, and hermeneutics to be a question of what the text means. The conflation is de Man's attempt at mediation I spoke about, but fails because of the history we are looking at, when it has been assumed that the way a text is arranged is also its meaning (rather than entertaining notions of 'content' [another concept fallen by the wayside] the emphasis is on structure). We can give a temporary conclusion and say once again that meaning has gone over into the realm of the social, that it resides in the reader, or more precisely, in the interaction between reader and text in the hermeneutic circle. Whilst dealing with arguments that assert immanence, we have noted that, contrary to their own assertions, the whole movement thus far in the history of intention has been towards this social realm, whether regarded in some way as homogeneous, as in such phrases as 'the sharability of meaning'; or as heterogeneous and possibly discrete, as in de Man's hermeneutic circles, which may or may not (de Man is unclear) be sharable.

Knapp and Michaels

If we now move from 1967 to 1982, the second fifteen-year cycle jump, we find intention once again raising its head when an article by Steven Knapp and Walter Benn Michaels in *Critical Inquiry* rekindles the flames of the argument.[34] The arguments are collected in the book *Against Theory: Literary Studies and the New Pragmatism*.[35] I pointed out that de Man never makes clear the relation between intention and meaning. In Knapp and Michaels's argument, the relation is very clear: for them it is nonsensical to conceive of meaning without intention. W. J. T. Mitchell's introduction to *Against Theory* places Knapp and Michaels neatly into the history of intention this chapter has so far narrated:

> Historicists like Hirsch think that we find meaning by ascertaining intention; formalists like Wimsatt and Beardsley (and, more recently, Paul de Man) think that meaning will take care of itself if we 'subtract' extrinsic intention and let the language of the text work on us.[36]

Mitchell claims that unlike Wimsatt and Beardsley, Knapp and Michaels are quite indifferent to where intention is found. Quoting from Mitchell's introduction again: 'Their only claim is that, interpretation, the finding of meaning, just *is* the finding of intention. To look for one is to look for the other, because they are just the same thing.'[37] They illustrate it by using what has become known as 'the wave poem'. They imagine someone walking along a beach. The stroller notices some squiggles in the sand which turn out to be the following:

> A slumber did my spirit seal;
> I had no human fears:
> She seemed a thing that could not feel
> The touch of earthly years.

According to Knapp and Michaels the person may 'understand what the words mean', recognise it as writing and even as a poem, without needing to think about the author. Now a wave comes along and leaves beneath these lines the following:

> No motion has she now, no force;
> She neither hears nor sees;
> Rolled around in earth's diurnal course
> With rocks, and stones, and trees.[38]

There are now two possibilities. Either it is purely accidental, or the pedestrian ascribes 'these marks to some agent capable of intentions (the living sea, the haunting Wordsworth, etc.)'.[39] If it is accidental, although it might seem like poetry, it clearly is not, because it is not language, for to deprive the words of an author 'is to convert them into accidental likenesses of language. They are not, after all, an example of intentionless meaning; as soon as they become intentionless they become meaningless as well'.[40]

So for Knapp and Michaels meaning without intention is a nonsense, some author is always involved, though not necessarily the signing author. And for them it is not a question of looking for intention in order to find the meaning, if you look for one you are necessarily seeking the other. By the way, the broader argument of their article is that the whole mistake of theory to date has been a belief that they *can* be separated.

Summary

In the framework I have constructed for the history of intention we have apparently gone from one extreme to the other, from Wimsatt and Beardsley's claim that an appeal to intention is fallacious, to Knapp and Michaels's claim that any notion of meaning *without* intention is illogical. But this does not appear to help us. I intimated at the start that the pot of gold would consist of finding a means of tracking down intention, which would then enable us to fix meaning. We have found both in Knapp and Michaels, but they tell us here and in 'A Reply to Our Critics' that it is 'fool's gold', as the following quotation illustrates:

> In our view, the object of all reading is always the historical author's intention, even if the historical author is the universal muse. That's why we don't think it makes sense to *choose* historical intention – and why we don't think it's possible to choose any kind of intention.[41]

And to crown the uselessness of this expedition to find the pot of gold at the end of the rainbow and the whole of this chapter's historical project:

To insist, as we do, that the object of interpretation is always a historical intention is, once again, not to justify or even to recommend the pursuit of historical scholarship. Textual editors, historical scholars, New Critical explicators, and everyone else – from the standpoint of intention – are all doing the same thing. Since it provides no help in choosing among critical procedures, the idea of intention is methodologically useless.[42]

So intention *is* fundamentally related to meaning, but *so* fundamentally it does not help. Or does it? My interest in Knapp and Michaels is their claim that we cannot escape the idea of intention, nor can we escape the idea of an author, and note, it is *'an* author', not *the* author. For them it is theoretically and practically useless. It has no consequences because it cannot help us decide which methodology to use. That is fair enough; but it does have consequences in that we can attempt to re-introduce the notion of an author and intention into our studies of meaning.

Before I do that however, let us imagine that everybody in the history of intention has been right, right in their descriptions but not in the claims for consequences. These positions could be formulated thus:

1. It is not possible to know what the author had in mind, what his or her intentions were (Wimsatt and Beardsley, de Man)
2. Meaning, language and literature are all socially determined, lie in the social realm (Wimsatt and Beardsley, de Man, Hirsch, Knapp and Michaels)
3. Texts are semantically autonomous (Wimsatt and Beardsley, de Man)
4. There is no meaning without intention (Hirsch, Knapp and Michaels)
5. Texts are unified only in the hermeneutic circle (de Man)
6. Meaning and significance (that is, interpretation and evaluation [criticism]) are separate and separable (Hirsch)
7. To know that intention = meaning is methodologically useless in choosing amongst critical procedures (Knapp and Michaels).

First of all, there is no meaning without some kind of intention, the two are fundamentally related. It is also correct for Knapp and Michaels to say that intention can be found in many areas, the author, textual history, implied speakers, the autonomous text as intentional object (as de Man envisages it), and here we can introduce other terms that function as 'authors': the Freudian/Lacanian/Kristevan subconscious; gender; deconstruction; and ideology. All the terms authorise the meanings they generate in some way (for example the workings of 'the psyche' explain and generate the psychological and/or psychoanalytic meanings) and thus become the authors of those interpretations. In all these areas the text *means* something, and that meaning is linked to the intention to mean, whichever arena is chosen. If I want to interpret the text, and believe meaning resides with the author, I will try to find out what he or she intended using a range of possible material. I will seek other evidence beside the text, as Wimsatt and Beardsley know, as Hirsch knows, as Knapp and Michaels know. I will have to accept that I will only ever know what it probably means, as Hirsch points out, because, just like any theory, it can never be proved but only disproved. However, you might disagree with my approach and argue that to believe in an author's intentions is to subscribe to an outmoded humanist ideology and that the text is the result of social forces, or social modes of production. Whatever the intention found here in the social arena becomes the author of the text's meaning. And so on. We might say that some approaches work negatively. For example, deconstruction, some psychoanalytical and some Marxist (Althusserian) approaches seek to find meaning in the lacunae, in what was not intended, or put another way, in what was intended to be repressed. Here we have the intentions of the conscious/subconscious, the intentions of patriarchy, the intentions of the class matrix. And I think Knapp and Michaels are right, there is nothing intrinsically and logically here to say that one methodology is better than another. All of these approaches theoreticians, students and critics have found perfectly valid and useful ways into texts at one time or another.

The Object of Study

This brings me on to a much larger issue in which I think intention is inextricably bound. The reason why we cannot adjudicate between the numerous theories, criticisms and methodologies is simple: there is no theoretical or practical consensus as to what the object of study is or how to constitute it, nor how to constitute the discipline known as Literature. It would be enough for some to take the pluralist line and say it is a mixture of all of these approaches and theories. For some, like Tony Bennett in *Outside Literature*, English Literature is purely an ideological construct that should be reconstructed as a subject that can set exercises which can be objectively examined, instead of depending upon humanist assumptions and using the subject of English Literature as a moral tool to instil the 'correct' societal values in students.[43] For Antony Easthope, in his *Literary Studies into Cultural Studies*, literary studies is anyway dissolving into the study of signifying practices, since the Leavisite legacy of the high culture/popular culture divide, upon which literary studies is predicated, is no longer tenable.[44] For literary studies he would substitute a cultural studies which would analyse Joseph Conrad's *Heart of Darkness*, Edgar Rice Burroughs's *Tarzan*, a Benson and Hedges advertisement, and an 1812 knitter's song side-by-side. In this larger argument meaning and intention are either real gold or fool's gold, since they will always enable you to display your framework of interpretation, but refuse you any grounds for adjudicating between yours and anyone else's. It will all depend upon what economy of Literature we want to set up.

What does D. H. Lawrence's *The Rainbow* mean? And what is the difference between studying the meaning of that novel and the news item at the beginning of this paper? I can subject either to the same critical methodologies: gender, ideology, psychoanalysis, reader-response, Marxist, Formalist, New Historicist. So what is the difference? My theory and practice at that juncture would not help me differentiate. Or do they mean in different ways? This may be nearer the mark, and I would say this: that when we study Literature we assume there is an intention behind what we choose to study, and that intention would have to be described as an attempt to engage life in an artistic mode, we assume that there is an artistic intention – even if we are unable to define what that means to everyone's satisfaction. However, we understand this 'artistic intention' as different from the newspaper article. Nor should 'artistic intention' be taken as synonymous with the aesthetic, since artistic intention does not in itself indicate how a particular artist or group of artists interpreted what it means to be art. It is simply enough to say that we are under the sign of artistic intention – and this, like other 'intentions' can be located in a number of places (the psyche – a desire to express, be creative, communicate, catharsis; society – the aesthetic ordering of ideology, the reproduction and naturalisation of societal dynamics), but can be separated out from other modes (soup can labels, newspaper articles). This is to take the Knapp and Michaels argument one stage further; if there is no meaning without intention, there is no artistic meaning without artistic intention. That is the only way we can begin to say that Lawrence's *The Rainbow* is different from the news item, its intention is different. It begs the question of how art and Literature are to be viewed, and what we believe the intention is behind the production of them, but just to be able to put it in these terms is to claim that the study of Literature is different from the study of 'signifying practices' or 'cultural studies', since it presumes a literary intention. And as Hirsch says, we can never ascertain to the point of verification what an intention is, but we can ascertain to varying degrees of probability. We also proceed as if there is an artistic intention, whatever we perceive the case to be, otherwise there is no art, it would be as nonsensical as 'intentionless meaning'. If we see it as desirable that we should be able to mark out the boundaries of Literature, then that is where we must start. And whilst it is perfectly feasible that semiotics, deconstruction, Marxisms, poststructuralisms, feminisms, linguistics etc. can be accommodated in such a conception of Literature or Literary Studies, they are neither necessary nor sufficient to delimit the subject area, though there may be a desire to incorporate them. The use of intention both to fix meanings and the nature of the object must surely be the only way we can do this.

I can see that this is not likely to please a good many people. In effect I am saying that a Marxist will only obtain Marxist meanings; a feminist, feminist meanings, and so on. In other words, the meaning found will be the meaning for whichever methodology is used. I would like to make a tentative start as to how we might proceed out of these tautological theoretical approaches (reminiscent of de Man's hermeneutic circularity), although it risks seeming old-fashioned and even recidivist.

Let us use the following analogy. Imagine a glass. What is it? We can describe it in many different ways, ways which can be subdivided into various disciplines – chemistry, physics, fine arts. The nature of the object reciprocally delimits along with the discipline which descriptive methodologies or theories are applicable. Meteorology would be of little use here, a consequence both of the nature of the glass and the nature of the discipline. It is obvious that there is no one single true definition of the glass, and no one true single approach which could approach such a state of affairs. Now imagine we want to set up a discipline called 'Glass Studies', or 'Glassology'. How are we going to define Glassology? The study of glasses? Yet we can say that there is nothing intrinsic to the nature of a glass which could define the study of it, just as we might acknowledge the artificiality of the *discipline* English Literature. The problem for glassology is that, as already pointed out, we have no single definition of 'a glass', since it can be described in a variety of ways, a situation we can take as analogous to the various theoretical approaches in Literature. And at some point someone is bound to argue that we cannot theoretically justify talking about a glass as a receptacle when the same material exists in the world as a receptacle like a bowl, which has certain similarities to a glass, and then an ashtray, and perhaps even a window, just as the study of Literature cannot at present theoretically separate the study of a novel from the study of a newspaper article – they are both species of writing, just as a window and an ashtray may both be species of glass.

This points up a couple of things. On the most basic level what has happened is that students of Literature, which includes critics, lecturers and theorists, assume the study of Literature to *be* Literature, to constitute it. Yet Literature does not depend, in the sense of a one-on-one causal relationship, upon the *study* of it, just as a glass cannot be said to depend upon 'Glassology' for its existence. But we can deduce that Literature is 'meaning' dependent, and that that means 'intention' *is* involved (where we choose to locate it is up to us, but we cannot conceive of it *without* meaning). Inextricably linked with this meaning is the assumption of an author, and once again, where we choose to locate the author – in the historical being, in society, gender, a psyche, textual unity – is arbitrary in the sense that none of the related theories or approaches can ground itself to the extent that it can *necessarily* preclude other theories or approaches. Even the most abstract theories, such as a Formalist approach that would reduce poetry to rhyme schematics, are positing some relation to meaning as the overriding factor ('defamiliarisation' – how to 'see' or apprehend something that has become familiar is to grant meaning). Nor does it seem, at this stage, that mediation is actually the problem as conceived at the beginning of the book. The problem exists because theories of Literature (and art) cannot logically posit objects that are both transcendent and contingent. As we have seen, theories relating to 'the author' and 'intention', no matter which side of the divide of the sociohistorical/immanent theoretical axis they place themselves, have been unable to avoid precisely the mediation that undermines their own theoretical premises. It seems then that despite the continual theoretical division into opposing forces this separation between the two camps is theoretically untenable. This is further explored in the next chapter.

4
Well and Truly Fact: Postmodernism and History[1]

I speculated in the Introduction whether a venture such as this book should bear the traces of its own history, or erase them in favour of organising all of the material around what is already known by the author to be a conclusion. This is an argument that can be aligned with the structure versus event debate which was also sketched in the Introduction. Rather than set out the problem in these terms, however, I would like to look at the issue as it has been transmuted within the discourse on postmodernism, since it is here that explorations of history and knowledge have been at their most acute. It can also be claimed that the postmodernism versus history debate is actually another form of the immanent versus contingent divide so far described.

A fundamental problem for the book as it acknowledges the force of the arguments of postmodernist theory is self-consciousness. Here the self can be understood as either the author's knowledge of himself or the reification of the book into a self-conscious artefact. To put it in terms of the postmodern debate, the issue is whether there is a critical space from which to know something that is not already compromised. Because the book has attempted to place itself at the cutting-edge, as the latest intervention into the debate, there is an obvious need to know where it stands in relation to (literary) 'theory' in general and the current debate surrounding it. Yet the whole project of achieving some kind of closure through the mediation of immanence-based and socio-historical theories suggests that the book actually wants to place itself at the end of theory. Perhaps this is what de Man means when he claims that 'the resistance to theory is theory itself', for if the book were to be successful, it would result in the removal of the need for any further theory, theoretically at least. To believe or state that the required mediation was the one to end all theory would be hubris on my part. But if it is not to be hubris, that is, if I am not to hold out the belief that I am engaged in a rational argument that can be carried on regardless of circumstance and that can carry its correctness beyond contingency, I am left with the problem that I am situated in a mode of Fish-style pragmatism, of doing what I do, of saying what I say, simply because of the community I find myself in. The book thus becomes, no matter how well or badly argued, a question of belief rather than validation. Just what is it possible to do with theory? Put another way, how is this book to know itself?

Unfortunately, the status of 'postmodernism' itself presents a problem. If I take it that 'postmodernism' is everywhere, that in fact I am (we are) all living in the postmodern age and thoroughly imbued with its épistème, which we may or may not be able to describe depending upon our theory of 'self-consciousness', then there is not even the space for an argument. For the moment I will assume that postmodernism is a discourse and as such a very useful conceptual tool, but that the pre-eminence it often claims for itself cannot be taken as a given. Rather than leave this assertion as a statement of belief, I will discuss the problem as I see it with 'postmodernism', and I think that the major fault-line here *is* 'history'. It seems to me that one place where postmodernism has gained very little ground is in this very discipline. Not surprising, perhaps, since postmodernism is often taken to herald the end of history. Whilst postmodern theory in its rush to claim the demise of metanarratives and linear time displays an obvious antagonism to notions of history, there may be a very good reason for the antagonism which does not necessarily depend upon the resistance of historians.

The fate of history in postmodernism is well-described by Steven Connor when he summarises Fredric Jameson's essay 'Postmodernism and Consumer Society':

> The key that connects the leading features of postmodern society ... to the schizoid pastiche of postmodernist culture is the

fading of a sense of history. Our contemporary social system has lost its capacity to know its own past, has begun to live in 'a perpetual present' without depth, definition, or secure identity.[2]

It is the case that postmodernism would rather not be *in* history. It is thus no wonder that critics and adherents of postmodernism who depend upon it in some way, have a vested interest in declaring, as they so often have, 'the end of history'. Once they allow the notion of 'history' as a still viable discourse, postmodernism itself becomes a contingent concept which will inevitably be superseded. Without the end of history we cannot have the beginning of postmodernism as it likes to present itself. It is therefore ironic that a phenomenon that has often proclaimed 'the end of history', through critics such as Andreas Huyssen, Fredric Jameson and Hal Foster,[3] should have such a temporal landmark as 'post' in its rubric. Yet if history is narrative, and this is how I shall portray it at its most desirable, then the very word 'postmodernism' cannot avoid being in history, and history in a teleological sense, with postmodernism acting as the telos. Although postmodernism is commonly seen as a continuous opening-up leading to a vista of endless possibilities, it does so at the cost of positing itself as *the* master narrative, able to see itself as the fated closure of culture, society, and, of course, history. This can hardly be said to be an opening-up on its own part. My distrust with this line of discourse of postmodernism, which I would suggest is fairly mainstream, is that it sets up the concept 'history' in a specific discursive field which it believes it can exempt itself from. The paradox is that postmodernism can claim to be outside history, because, historically speaking, it is at the end of history.

At the 'Literature and the Contemporary' conference at Hull University, 23-24 March 1994, Thomas Docherty dismissed the common understanding I am portraying here (the 'mainstream') as an appropriation of the least likely form of postmodernism, that is, the Rorty strand of antifoundationalism. He went on to promote a postmodernism that gave attention to the 'thinginess' of events, most likely unknowable in their 'thisness'. Yet such an argument can hardly be said to avoid the pitfalls of postmodernism as described in this chapter since it refuses to make links between events.[4] Docherty (on evidence at the conference) also represents a trend to define postmodernism not in terms of a time period but rather as a mood, a move which allows us to detect as being active postmodernists living at any time since the year dot. It is an approach which, I believe, does away with the usefulness of the concept 'postmodernism' whilst colluding with that aspect of postmodernism Jameson identifies as leading to a flattening of historical perspective – for it presents a levelling term to be applied consistently throughout the ages. In this way it actually works against Docherty's desire to respect the 'otherness'[5] of past events.

Our most everyday notion of history *is* as a narrative of the past. Jean-François Lyotard – one of the most widely drawn-upon commentators of postmodernism – has claimed that, at the simplest level, the postmodern can be defined as 'incredulity toward metanarratives'.[6] If this is the case, there are certain implications for history. If we cannot grasp our past in the form of a narrative that would explain it all, we cannot have history with a capital 'h'. Yes, there could be, following on from Lyotard, a whole spectrum of 'histories', perhaps called 'micronarratives', but we could lay no claim to fitting it into a larger narrative. According to this theory and methodology, we are able to achieve a narrative of a miners' strike at a local level, as it were, perhaps after the manner of Foucault, but we are not permitted to say that it is part of the ongoing struggle of the working class or a symptom of capitalism in crisis, as a vulgar Marxist narrative would have it. Such a miners' strike would be a discrete, discontinuous event. This approach to history is very evident in the ahistorical methodology of the New Historicism, which has been the fashionable fate of any notion of history. New Historicism can be described as Renaissance studies meets anthropology meets Foucault.[7] It typically explicates culture, society and events from minute particulars. One famous example of this is the description of a society which begins with a note left by Nietzsche to the effect 'I have left my umbrella', (for which definition see the back-page blurb of H. Aram Veeser's collection of critics' essays in *The New Historicism*).[8] This notion of particularity is perfectly at ease with postmodernism. It might even be a defining condition. In the New Historicism this archaeological, historicist outlook leads to a type of writing which provides cross-sections of societies and cultures frozen in time, thick descriptions of them at any one moment with no sense of before and after and no way of linking them, no way of providing a narrative thread. It is easy to see how this New Historicism, as a methodology, fits into the postmodern paradigm of a perpetual present, since these glances backwards to the past simply recover other presents, and in the process elide the dialectic between the past and the present (although even the idea of a dialectic is challenged by Elizabeth Ermarth in *Sequel to History: Postmodernism and the Crisis of Representational Time*.[9] I discuss this book later on in the chapter). The New Historical methodology is anti-narrative, and in many ways correlates with the predominantly empirical way of doing history which seems to dominate academia today as it strives to be a social science. But does it have to be this way? Do I really need a metanarrative of some kind just to be able to see a miners' strike in a wider framework, changing over time but linked to other factors? Am I constrained by my incredulity towards metanarratives? Should I not even consider knowledge in terms of 'events' such as 'miners' strikes'?

Before I discuss how this might affect our idea of history, I would like to state that I believe we *should* be incredulous towards metanarratives (again, an ethical injunction). But it is not the case, as Lyotard posits, that such incredulity can be widely observed, let alone be the common denominator for our postmodern age. All we need do is look at the rise of fundamentalism to scupper the idea. Or there are the problems in what used to be the Soviet Union, and what used to be Yugoslavia. The model metanarrative here is 'nationhood'. This particular metanarrative could be observed in the ready appeal made to patriotism in Britain at the time of the Falklands/Malvinas conflict (and, presumably, also in Argentina). The 'nation' is one of today's pre-eminent world-historical constructs. It might be objected that my idea of metanarrative is confused here, that the metanarratives of Marxism and Christianity relate every aspect of life to their descriptions and prescriptions, to the economic base or God's design, and that 'nationhood' hardly fits into that same order. I would argue however that it does, since who believes that a life can be lived outside the state? Is there anything we can do that is not circumscribed (surrounded) by the state? It defines us, positions us, and subjects us – in the sense that it makes us *its* subjects as well as 'subjecting us to' its demands. We might argue about the details, manifest in activities such as voting in a new government, the forcible removal of government, the mobilisation of one race against another, yet few ever propose hitching their destiny to anything other than the fate of a nation – its economy, its foreign policy, its cultural heritage and all the other constructs which presuppose a nation-state cannot be circumvented. The nation-state has its own supposed telos: greater happiness, greater wealth, greater justice. This is not to say that 'nationhood' is *the* meta-narrative everyone subscribes to – only fanatics subscribe to a metanarrative at every single level – yet we cannot *not* believe in the state. This is in exactly the same way that some people proclaim that we cannot *not* believe in God. Which leads me to wonder that if incredulity cannot be widely observed, just where is it that Lyotard has managed to locate it? This surely remains one of the problems in discussing postmodernism. We appear surrounded by it, yet so many of its defining characteristics and theoretical injunctions are given as statements of current fact: we live in a world of simulacra; we live in a world of an eternal present; we are incredulous towards metanarratives; we have lost our concept of linear (neutral, natural) time; we have lost all sense of a neutral, representational space. In theory these proclamations have reached the status of dogma; in practice confirming examples are memorable because so rare (are we really to take Baudrillard's assessment of the Gulf War as evidence of simulacra in the postmodern age?).

But this does not help. As I have already stated, I too am disbelieving in the face of grand historical schemes, schemes that try to fix me in their narratives without my consent – Marxism, religion, nationhood. Yet I retain the desire to understand miners' strikes, how science has changed, 'the rise of the novel', even the phenomenon we call postmodernism, but not as discrete, autonomous, hermetically-sealed events bearing no relation to anything outside of their own well-defined boundaries. The problem here does not lie with Lyotard's metanarratives, it lies with what has much more persuasive force in the discourse of postmodernism, the issue of legitimation (but also ethics, which I will broach later).

Postmodernism and History

How can I legitimate or give authority to one version of history, of, say, a miners' strike, over another? Let me go back to what I outlined as the possible consequence of doing away with meta-narrative paradigms, that is, 'histories', with small 'h's' and no way to choose between them. In postmodernism, every fact, all knowledge, is a function of the discourse that allows it, within which it is imbedded. Crudely put, I would have no way of judging between a Tory and a Labour version of a miners' strike. Each history would be correct within the limits of its own discourse. There is no place from which I could stand and pronounce judgement since I, too, would have to realise that my own pronouncement was a consequence of that particular discourse, that particular language game. Lyotard's argument is that this is because I can no longer appeal to, or rather, no longer believe in, a metanarrative. This is part of the larger postmodern philosophical picture, which, in a nutshell, poses the following riddle: What happens if there is no objective truth? Are we consigned to a crippling, enervating relativism? I would like to turn to the novel *Gravity's Rainbow* by Thomas Pynchon, and a commentary upon it, in order to illustrate just how all these forces come into play.[10]

Gravity's Rainbow, first published 1973, has often been taken as an exemplary postmodern text, if not *the* text. It is set in the Second World War and intermingles fact and fiction – if I can be allowed those distinctions for the present – in a slapstick manner. It gives a number of different explanations for the causes and continuation of the Second World War, Hitler not being one of them. These explanations include the paranoiac vision of 'a conspiracy' by 'Them' 'to defraud' and hide the truth;[11] the unfolding of a divine plan of predestination in which we may be the preterite (the passed over) or the elect;[12] a system of knowledge where what we can actually see is only a very small fraction of the whole of history that has been laid down;[13] a race between multinational technologies and business interests; the action of angels. The novel shows that the difficulty with history is not just a question of which version of the past is true, or how we can decide which is 'truer', but also of what paradigms for historical understanding we can possibly use when waiting in the wings is a postmodern discourse which threatens the very ideas of narrative, representation and time that a sense of history relies upon. It also raises the crisis some thinkers on history have taken on board, the problem of textuality. The novel gives the reader no clues as to which version of history, which metanarrative, is the correct one. Thus the novel is pluralist, or relativist, in its approach to history, and as such perfectly postmodern. It might be possible to argue that *Gravity's Rainbow* represents a folk memory, a collection of narratives that do not have to add up or stand the test of any rules of validation. In this sense it is the counter to official (academic) history. At this point in the chapter *Gravity's Rainbow* provides a possible approach for historical understanding, as 'history from the bottom up', a paradigm that answers some postmodern objections to history perceived as a discourse that does nothing more than allow 'the winners' to project a self-legitimating narrative. The main problem here, both for champions and detractors of postmodernism, is how to go some way to saying that some versions must needs be wrong, for example, how to say that the Second World War was not due solely to technological advancement or to the actions of angels.[14]

The difficulty with respect to the problem of adjudicating between alternative narratives is well illustrated when Brian McHale talks about Pynchon's novel.[15] After McHale has promoted postmodern fiction, including Pynchon's work, he says of *Gravity's Rainbow* that: 'it is lying to blame technologies or angels for the Second World War', and goes on to say, 'history is the record of real human action and suffering, and is not to be tampered with lightly'.[16] From nowhere McHale introduces ideas into the discourse of postmodernism that seem positively alien to it: human action; suffering; a responsibility to the past. McHale's contradictory reaction to *Gravity's Rainbow*'s understanding and narrativisation of the past is a prime instance of history emerging as postmodernism's fault-line. His valorisation of the postmodern sensibility – the coexistence of self-contained and incompatible worlds; a disregard for linear time and causality – undermines the ethical drive to understand the past historically. The pressing problem here is that historical discourse retains an ethical responsibility towards facts, whereas in the discursive field of postmodernism 'facts' have virtually no status. Realising this difficulty many proponents of postmodern theory will claim that of course there are facts, but they are problematical. However, they tend to remain so problematical that it is difficult to comprehend how they can be called 'facts' at all.[17] McHale states that 'one of the thrusts of postmodern revisionist history is to call into question the reliability of official history'.[18] McHale, like so many others, is precisely caught by the double-edged fictional transgression of official history. He understands that official history is (or may be) fictional, but nonetheless has to describe as 'lies' certain other, for him, impossible interpretations. In other words, he has to appeal to 'facts', and in doing so covertly appeals to some idea and ideal of what the Second World War really was, or to some current 'true' representation of it. At the same time is the realisation that all he can appeal to is the 'official' record, and that appeal itself is quite possibly an appeal to an alternative fiction. It is surely dishonest of proponents of postmodernism to assert antifoundational arguments, but when cornered by their own logic into confronting the lack of ethical responsibility this entails, sneak in through the back door some commitment to history and ethics, items which are in effect already so compromised by the make-up of postmodernism they are beyond redemption within the parameters of postmodernism. Yet surely Pynchon *is* right to challenge official versions of history.

Part of the problem lies in the proposed and supposed postmodern collapse of disciplines, in this case, the collapse of literature and history into one another, a consequence of the poststructuralist critique of textuality which results in an equating of the discourse of history with that of literature. Against this collapsing we can say that we cannot expect the discipline history, or at a more general and less technical level, historical understanding, to conform to the same rules, codes, conventions and regulations in which Literature as a discipline engages (and Literature here, interestingly, is confined predominantly to novels, since it is the pervasiveness of narrative that is at the heart of the matter, not the poetic or the dramatic, for instance). Simply because history and fiction are both narrative forms, this does not entail identical discourses. Fictional narratives and historical narratives have points of contact, but we should no more expect the collapse of one into another simply because they are both textually-based, on one level, or narrative-based, on another, any more than we could collapse football and basketball into each other because they both use a pitch, a spherical object, and two opposing teams. If we are looking for a ready-made cursor, we could say that history is accountable in a way that fiction is not. This is McHale's weak-spot – he believes in the postmodern collapse of literary and historical writing, yet still demands of a novel the same kind of accountability that any history of the Second World War would be subjected to. It is difficult to see, however, why once the two discursive modes are no longer separate anyone would expect any of the old criteria to be applicable. As Lionel Gossman points out, there are other distinctions to be made when literature and history are viewed as cultural practices. To quote a review of his book *Literature and History*, these are differences

> which can be located at the level of production (a historical text is expected to be based on methodical research), at the level of reception (a historical text is open to criticism), and at the level of cultural function (a historical text is expected to have a primarily cognitive, not aesthetic, function).[19]

I touched upon the fact that in the postmodern discursive field language itself, in the form of textuality, in the form of writing, has become problematical. We see this especially focused upon by poststructuralism, and in particular, deconstruction.[20] This has taken the form of creating an object of notorious indeterminacy – the Text. All writings, all texts, are, we now know, in the postmodern era, radically unstable. The repercussions for a discipline like history which depends for its material upon texts of all kinds are potentially horrendous. Its status would be that of writing about writing, which no doubt makes it doubly treacherous and meaningless. The facts of the past are non-existent – since if they come to us in the form of texts, we are once again on slippery ground. But how do texts and writing in general ever get to be such a thorny, intractable issue?

A typical manoeuvre to demonstrate how meaning cannot be fixed is to take a single sentence and subject it to a rigorous analysis which illustrates that it can be variously interpreted. The thinking behind this is that if we do not have the capacity to understand a simple sentence in a clear and an unambiguous manner, how can we expect to understand texts made up of larger units, paragraphs, chapters, books? Or the Text of the past. Yet, as critics point out more and more, this mode of thinking is faulty. The trick (don't blink) depends upon the denial of context. Remove anything from its context and it becomes the plaything of infinite signification. But allow back context and the possibility of less ambiguous explanation becomes increasingly available. We should recognise that it is the removal of context that is the jump into illusion and contrived ambiguity, not our sense of reference and context when faced with texts and the past. Surely to have greater context is to have greater understanding. Seen in this light, it is clear how postmodernism as I have described it works against our notion of history as a contextualisation of pasts and presents, and against our notion of history when it works with documents, what postmodernism would call a 'scene of writing' subject to all the vagaries of the text I have been talking about. We can reverse all this, and allow the more feasible scenario – that contexts are available and have the function of stabilising. There are now a number of consequences that do much to undercut the claims of postmodernism for itself.

One consequence relates directly to history. If context is taken into account postmodernism immediately becomes circumscribed, 'well and truly fact', we might say. Postmodernism can no longer proclaim itself *the* text, unstable, experiencing *jouissance* and an endless proliferation of meaning without any contextual grounding. In this version of postmodernism there is a constant spiralling away in what Steven Connor has identified as the sublime. Postmodernism asks us to do away with facts as something we can grasp and use, except of course the fact of postmodernism itself. But how does postmodernism know itself as postmodernism unless it has already contextualised itself, both chronologically (Docherty et al. notwithstanding), as I have already pointed out, and as a fact that has a potentially fixable meaning? The latter point is perhaps contestable in that the discourse of postmodernism often tries to mystify its own possible meaning. Commentators on postmodernism can be very keen to say that it cannot be defined, claiming that it is a conglomeration of characteristics that have no underlying common factor, or that discourse is always imbedded in what it describes, resulting in a kind of infinite regress. Unless, of course, as I am suggesting, we turn to history and context to arrest this bottomless, topless, sideless discourse upon discourse – and perhaps this most eminent variety of postmodernism *should* be charged for loitering without intent.

The problems with postmodernism and the avowed crises in epistemology and ontology are not really new, even if we have deigned to give them a new name. It is instead most likely the old chestnut of how we are to know ourselves. Rather than saying that this involves us in a discourse that gives up the ghost of rational argument and objective knowledge and automatically plunges us into the irrational, the subjective and other correlatives of Romanticism – itself seen as a drive towards transcending the temporal, the fixed, 'facticity', notions that have been opposed to the Enlightenment – instead of giving up that ghost, we could be saying that the past offers us the chance to know ourselves better than we do, or postmodernism would have us believe we can. Let us look more closely at two central features in our discussion of the nature of history and postmodernism.

TIME AND NARRATIVE

A common understanding of time is as a straight line over which events occur or unfold, although it would probably be stretching the point to claim that people regard this as strictly uniform, and therefore neutral. Concomitant with this understanding of time as linear is the belief in causality. A number of factors, scientific, cultural, political, have combined to put this understanding of time into question: the theory of Special Relativity; some feminist theory ('Woman's Time'); the fading away of industrial (factory) time for more flexible practices (David Harvey's post-Fordism); subjective experiences of time given validity (a minute can seem like an hour; the coextensive existence of memory of the past in present consciousness); mythical time. One of the major threats to a concept of history is the loss of 'cause-and-effect' that is predicated upon linear time. The particular problem is amply illustrated in *Gravity's Rainbow* where an opposition is set up between two characters who have different ideas of time and its relation to history. Pointsman represents the traditional view that one event happens after another in a chronological, causal sequence (point-by-point). This is how Pointsman the traditionalist describes the other character, Mexico, who represents what might be considered the post-war, and postmodern, view. Pointsman pleads:

> How can Mexico play, so at his ease, with these symbols of randomness and fright? Innocent as a child, perhaps unaware – perhaps – that in his play he wrecks the elegant rooms of history, threatens the idea of cause and effect itself. What if Mexico's whole *generation* have turned out like this? Will Postwar be nothing but 'events', newly created one moment to the next? No links? Is it the end of history?[21]

If our common-sense understanding of events through time as cause and effect goes, there can be no historical understanding. If we cannot explain events in terms of other events in a temporal fashion we have nothing, or rather, we would have what we get in the New Historicism, 'nothing but "events", newly created one moment to the next'.

We might turn Mexico's and postmodernist thinking back on itself by considering the implications of not looking for links. Is it not a failure of nerve to refuse the search for links, for causes? In fact, *Gravity's Rainbow*, as mentioned, gives us many possible links. It is possible to see an analogy with the problem of text and context I outlined at the start of the paper. Technology appears as one of the most likely explanations in *Gravity's Rainbow* for the Second World War. It has its own internal logic and drive. But it cannot explain everything. It requires other narratives. But I would suggest that this does not perforce entail that it be embraced by a metanarrative (a higher explanatory order) if its own narrative has insufficient explanatory power. Other narratives can conjoin since different narratives are obviously not necessarily mutually exclusive – they can be used to confirm. Nor need they be reconciled by some higher, validating narrative, just as the translation of one language into another does not require some universal metalanguage in order to validate the translation. In the light of a growing extreme-right aggression in Europe towards immigrant groups, in whose interest is it to declare that we cannot explain in any fashion a previous rise of fascism and its most likely causes?

One objection to my account of narrative contextualisation is this: what if the majority of people agree that the most likely cause of the Second World War *was* the action of angels? What if the majority of people accepted as true that the holocaust never happened and that it has all been a Jewish conspiracy? Our response is already there in the above, in that it would not be commensurable with the majority of other narratives available. The objection to this would be that we would not necessarily be operating on a logical level, so this response of adjudication between various narratives would not hold. A narrative cannot be objectively, scientifically true (although this is the old concept of scientific truth) the argument would go, and so if enough people regard it as factual that the holocaust did not happen there is no higher appeal than this consensual truth. But then the majority of people would be operating in a way that is not comprehensible to current modes of thought. It would be to operate out of context. Choose any particular text (cause) and isolate it from its context and it will appear unstable. Contextualise and the material (possible causes) become more plausible or implausible. Thus, taken in isolation, 'angels' as an explanation has an inner logic as a cause of the Second World War, but alongside other narratives and possible causes cannot be sustained.

Another way of looking at time in the postmodern matrix also does away with the idea of linearity and 'historical time'. According to Ermarth:

> postmodern narrative language undermines historical time and substitutes for it a new construction of temporality that I call rhythmic time. This rhythmic time either radically modifies or abandons altogether the dialectics, the teleology, the transcendence, and the putative neutrality of historical time; and it replaces the Cartesian *cogito* with a different subjectivity whose manifesto might be Cortázar's 'I swing, therefore I am'.[22]

Further on Ermarth claims: 'In postmodern narratives temporality has little to do with historical conventions; instead it is multivalent and non-linear.'[23] But there is a problem with the whole concept of Ermarth's postmodern project as it takes in postmodern textuality, postmodern time and postmodern subjectivity. She talks as if people experience time in the way she suggests ('I swing, therefore I am'), yet acknowledges that popular narratives and narrative strategies continue to view time as nineteenth-century novelists did.[24] Her argument therefore is that in a certain type of narrative called 'postmodern' there is a tendency to do away with linear, historical thinking. For this to have consequences for culture, 'the subject', history, time, events, as she suggests, it would require that people actually experience time in relation to historical understanding in this way. But as she and so many others point out, history is a particular discourse and a particular construct, it is a way of understanding. Ermarth et al. on the one hand perform the postmodern/poststructuralist manoeuvre of exposing the linguistic/tropic/discursive nature of an old paradigm as if the fact that something is 'discourse' automatically invalidates it. There *are* other notions of time, and some of these can be explored in relation to history (as this chapter briefly sketches later on), but to argue that we (should) experience time in one way which is believed to be the natural (real! true!) way (the 'I swing' etc. mode) is to relapse into the dogma that has been exposed.

One of the problems with Ermarth's analysis is that it assumes a type of thinking that cannot comprehend history as an ongoing process (negotiation, circulation) between past, present and future. Like a Pointsman or a Mexico, she sets up a singular paradigm of history that does not do justice to the diverse notions of time and history that might be used. For example, people can feel themselves 'inside history', a notion that does not conform to Pointsman's, Mexico's or Ermarth's paradigms. A recent event provides us with an example.

Wednesday 16 September 1992, was an extraordinary day in the global foreign exchange market when the Bank of England spent upwards of £15 billion in a futile attempt to maintain the value of sterling. Barclays Bank estimated a £30 billion turnover in its own foreign exchange (forex) department – 'more than the Bank of England holds in foreign reserves'.[25] The comments of Doug Bate on that day, chief trader at Barclays, London's biggest forex department, illustrate how people experience 'the swing' (as

Ermarth puts it), whilst also illustrating that this is not necessarily an abandonment of historical time (as Ermarth sets it up). 'On Wednesday, I felt as though we were all a part of history, and it was great to be a part of it. We have just had a week of historical importance, and it was wonderful to be involved in making it all happen.'[26] Who did not feel that they were witnessing 'historical events', 'historical time' even, when the Berlin Wall fell, or when Ceaucescu was ousted? This certainly may be a phenomenon of the postmodern age, made possible by a technology that allows the world to witness events as they happen, but does this diminish or increase our 'sense of history'? Is not the current anguish at the rise of anti-immigrant and anti-Semitic sentiment caused by our very sense of history, by our very knowledge that it bears comparison with past events? If I understand Ermarth correctly, the 'swing' she talks about is precisely this conjunction of past, present and future that is one paradigm of historical understanding.

The events on Wednesday 16 September 1992 are exemplary in another way. They show the difficulty of constructing history based upon nation-states. If there is a change in historical sensibility due to the questions of metanarratives that postmodernism raises, then this is surely one arena where it can operate to good effect. Our sense of the importance of nation-states as the referents of historical understanding are outmoded when a Bank has a greater turnover than the foreign reserves of the country within which it operates and goes a great way to altering economic policy of that country to suit its own needs. If we are to understand 'events' we need to rethink event-spaces, and not, as postmodern theory tries to do, create a time-space compression that flattens events into a single time-space experience of the present. Of course, the concept of nation-states is far from dead, as already stated. But in order to understand changes it is perhaps the wrong category with which to map out the past, present and future. For example, although the splintering of nation-states into smaller nation-states (USSR, Yugoslavia) is often done under the guise and appeal of some notion of nationhood, to trace the causes of these changes the event-space of the nation-state would seem the inappropriate place with which to do it.

Having delivered a polemic against postmodernism, it is now my turn to rescue it in some way. Firstly I feel myself to be a product, for better or worse, of some of the traits that go to make up postmodernism. Most obviously, I find myself pronouncing upon the discipline of 'History' when I have very little grounding in it, holding it up, it must seem, as *the* refutation of postmodernism as the current period descriptor. More subtly, perhaps, I have approached the whole issue in a manner which suggests the eclectic particularity I have already commented upon. I have attacked each perceived assault by postmodernism on history at a local level. Thus narrative, representation, time and the status of knowledge have been addressed within terms which rescue them *for* history, without resorting to any single concept of history I might have that would embrace and integrate all these areas. I will now switch to some broad strokes that leave the nitty-gritty particularity of details behind.

One question I raised but never fully answered was the issue of legitimation. This might be rephrased as 'Who has the authority for the historical stories we are asked to believe are true?' The answer is the state, or the state in the form of the intellectual state apparatuses. But does that not imply that all history will be official history? Pynchon's book shows that an official history will always presuppose counter-histories, secret histories. It is always a fight for the right to tell stories, to invest those stories with the necessary authority, sometimes through negotiation, sometimes through outright confrontation. Does that mean giving up the ideal of rationality, of being able to choose on reasonable grounds between conflicting narratives of the past? No. Once again, such a yielding would only be on ground that desired some *absolute* meta-knowledge and could not find it. The problem of 'the absolute' is dealt with in the next chapter.

If we do want our history to be narrative and yet avoid the old chestnut of reprehensible subjectivity, an objection might be raised in the form of the question: 'Can narratives be rational?' Probably not. The possibility of cause-and-effect covering laws, the type of law that says if there is a certain factor a in existence it will always be a necessary and sufficient condition for b to occur, is unlikely. Nor is it likely that less rigorous 'laws' can be operable where narratives are concerned. Should we therefore ditch narrative and stick to the analytic-style of doing history which aims to be a science and provides such details as the amount of steel exported from Sweden between 1920 and 1930 and little else? That seems, as such, a narrowing and a defeat. It can be useful, but surely only if we put it into a larger framework of narrativisation.

Again: can historical narrative be rational? No, but it can be a form of understanding, and there can be a commensurability between narratives that allows for accountability.

This all seems a long way from postmodernism, although of course the discussion of history here is always circumscribed by postmodernism, or so postmodernism would have us believe. But what if postmodernism has got it all wrong and it is history, not postmodernism, that is in the ascendant and further that, rather than the death of the épistème 'history' with the onslaught of postmodernism, postmodernism is alive as a discourse but itself circumscribed by the épistème it would do away with? To answer that I would like to move back on to the more familiar ground of fiction and a couple of ideas taken from Martin Amis's novel *London Fields*.[27] My first quotation from the book suggests an ascendancy for historical sensibility in the postmodern world rather than a demise:

> We used to live and die without any sense of the planet getting older, of mother earth getting older, living and dying. We used to live outside history. But now we're all coterminous. We're inside history now all right, on its leading edge, with the wind ripping past our ears.[28]

In other words, the postmodern sensibility that attempts to define where we are at now is not a sublime existence of groundless, timeless, endless play and signification, it is the exact opposite, a real sense of our own closure, the sense of an ending (a very looking into the face of death that Ermarth claims 'history' avoids and postmodernism embraces). Rather than look to an incredulity towards metanarratives, is not the discourse of ecology and responsibility to the planet more the order of the postmodern day, framed by a sense of the whole planet's temporality, contingency and material existence?

The second quotation from *London Fields*:

> Perhaps because of their addiction to form, writers always lag behind the contemporary formlessness. They write about an old reality, in a language that's even older. It's not the words: it's the rhythms of thought. In this sense all novels are historical novels.[29]

It is interesting that Amis, like Ermarth, points to 'rhythm' as a key to understanding, but that this rhythm is precisely the key toward historical understanding. It seems to me that the discourse of postmodernism is exactly this attempt to grasp the contemporary, as Connor points out in his introduction to *Postmodernist Culture*. Baudrillard's idea of simulacra is the exemplary move in this case: of course he and other critics of his ilk will find that things appear as copies without originals if their main desire is to describe things as they are now, with an approach that uses a synchronic paradigm rather than allowing a historical context. The double-edgedness of writing and of signs that postmodernism (and poststructuralism in particular) has identified does not make the possibility of historical discourse doubly treacherous, it simply enables us to realise that the past is being re-presented through specific discursive strategies.

I have discussed history mainly in relation to the past. Much of the use-value of history however, as well as providing a possible standpoint from which we can gain a greater self-knowledge, is often taken to be bound up with a future. If postmodernism seeks to proclaim the end of history, or use it for its own ends in a way which denies any grounding for historical understanding outside of postmodernism, it does so by also denying us any notion of the future. We might ask: 'What will postmodernism look like from a future standpoint?' Just as postmodernism has difficulty with that aspect of history we denote as the past, it is a condition of the possibility of discourse upon postmodernism that it has no space for this question either, of whether there is a life after postmodernism. From the point of view of this book, it can be seen that postmodernism has posited and positioned itself as a synchronic and autonomous discourse, that is, one that believes in immanence rather than context (in this case history). It would certainly not be pushing the point too far to claim that at the theoretical level postmodernist theory, as with those theories discussed in the previous two chapters, cannot sustain itself. Only by falsely circumscribing its own claims can it avoid the mediation that this book seeks.

ETHICS

If one theme running through this chapter has been postmodernism's unwillingness to accept its own historical status, another has been the ethical dimension. In whose interest is it to forgo a sense of history and historical understanding? This can be put into the postmodern nexus as illustrated below.

Nineteen ninety-four began with a most enjoyable farce entitled 'Back to Basics'. Its author was the British Prime Minister John Major and it grew out of an original idea put to him by Barbara Cartland, quite appropriately, since, as most people know, she is a writer of improbable Romantic fiction. During the most entertaining period of the furore, when Conservative MPs David Ashby and Tim Yeo successfully played their parts, an unnamed Tory colleague predicted the following: 'The damage may not be insuperable if things start to go right. It's astonishing how in the past we were able to win elections really quite soon after being in difficulties with Westland and the poll tax. Memories are quite short.'[30] Such casual cynicism is depressing. It is perfectly in accord with the assessment of politics provided by Milan Kundera's *The Book of Laughter and Forgetting*. The novel shows how politics is a constant, selective forgetfulness, or, as the character Mirek in the book says, 'the struggle of man against power is the struggle of memory against forgetting'.[31] The novel itself has enough characteristics to be called postmodern, and if we are to believe the blurb on the back of the book, our experience of reading the novel will mirror the book's own hedonism and lack of political concern. This marketing assessment is perfectly in keeping with the prepolitical-correctness school of postmodernism, lest we forget, the postmodernism that took part in the heady sixties of 'happenings', 'hippies', subversion and promiscuous sex, the kind of outlook that underwrites the desire for postmodern texts to be subversive and irreverent. But discussion of postmodernism has undergone

Postmodernism and History

a change in more years as it tries to attach itself to political correctness and responsibility. It is not just politicians who rely upon short memories, academics are also guilty. But given the force of postmodern objections to assertions of fact, the apparent groundlessness of concepts such as 'history', how would it be possible to promote an ethics that avoided a paralysing relativism and provided some kind of grounding for a notion of 'history'? I would like to tentatively suggest the following.

> On the march to work, limping in our large wooden shoes on the icy snow, we exchanged a few words, and I found out that Resnyk is Polish; he lived twenty years at Paris but speaks an incredible French. He is thirty, but like all of us, could be taken for seventeen or fifty. He told me his story, and today I have forgotten it, but it was certainly a sorrowful, cruel and moving story; because so are all our stories, hundreds of thousands of stories, all different and all full of a tragic, disturbing necessity. We tell them to each other in the evening, and they take place in Norway, Italy, Algeria, the Ukraine, and are simple and incomprehensible like the stories in the Bible. But are they not themselves stories of a new Bible?[32]

Primo Levi's book on his time in Auschwitz is another reminder of our need for history, to recount these stories, as Levi himself does, to bear witness. It is an ethical injunction. The recurring dream Levi has in the extermination camp is of telling his family and friends of his experience only to find that no one is listening. When he shares his dream with others in the camp he discovers that everyone has the same fear: that people are indifferent to their stories. I would suggest that it is the holocaust that provides us with our grounding for history, demands that we retain our sense of history, that we attempt to understand our past *because of* the holocaust. Moreover, the holocaust presents us, albeit negatively, with a telos – that it must never happen again. If the holocaust narratives do indeed provide a new beginning, the future is shaped by our own fear that another holocaust might occur and that our ethical responsibility is at all costs to prevent it.

I realise the problems with such an ethical base: the holocaust, as Thomas Keneally has suggested, is a European problem; the holocaust belongs to Jewish history; the meaning or significance or importance of the holocaust is far from clear. There are no logical responses to these objections. If the difficulty is that a sense of world history rather than a Eurocentric history is required, we might point to systematic genocide elsewhere in the twentieth century. I am sure that from a postmodern viewpoint it would be possible to argue that none of this counts as a rebuttal to groundlessness. But it seems to me clear that the logic or rationality or reasoning or performance of postmodern discourse is not the correct beginning. These events demand a historical awareness, demand that stories be heard. That is the ethical context from which to begin, in the future, any discussion of postmodernism and history. We might take the following eloquent testimony from Levi as a warning:

> For living men, the units of time always have a value, which increases in ratio to the strength of the internal resources of the person living through them; but for us, hours, days, months spilled out sluggishly from the future into the past, always too slowly, a valueless and superfluous material, of which we sought to rid ourselves as soon as possible. With the end of the season when the days chased each other, vivacious, precious and irrecoverable, the future stood in front of us, grey and inarticulate, like an invincible barrier. For us, history had stopped.[33]

What can be concluded is that in the current drive of postmodern thought, geared towards an ahistorical belief in the immanence and sublimity of current existence (the 'now', the 'contemporary', radical otherness), the past, and therefore the unknowability and unrepresentability of past events, the view from this side of the divide is challenged not on theoretical grounds (as in the past two chapters) but according to ethical demands. Such an assessment looks forward to Part II and illustrates that mediation might have to incorporate non-theoretical understandings.

Another failure of postmodernism has been that in the face of relativism and pluralism – its defining characteristics – it has been unable to tackle the question of value (like the question of ethics above), other than to say it is, like everything else in the postmodern environment, contingent and relative (postmodern theory's own 'mediation' between the two camps is thus the double-think of describing everything that comes within its remit as local and discrete, that is, everything except itself). As with textually-based knowledge, as much of history is, the notion of value has been placed under considerable stress by postmodern theory, yet, as the next chapter shows, just as with 'intention', 'the author', and '(con)text', the current attacks are themselves fundamentally flawed.

5
About Value

It might be conceded that, despite the supporting convictions provided in the Introduction and elsewhere in the book, 'meaning' is not so central to literary theory as has been suggested. So rather than look at aspects of interpretation, which, as Steven Connor confirms in *Theory and Cultural Value*, has been the major preoccupation of virtually all theory and criticism over the past twenty-odd years, we might turn from issues integral to hermeneutics such as 'author' and 'intention' and approach Literature from the perspective of 'value'.

How might this chapter proceed? It might split value into three areas: use-value, exchange-value and pleasure-value. This would be a reasonable way to begin a chapter on Literature, value and evaluation, systematically placing Literature in each of the categories. It might go on to claim that Literature was a mixture of all three value-categorisations, and then go on to examine them in the context of culture. Yet there is a certain inevitability about doing this, just as with the chapters on 'author' and 'intention' there is an inevitability about which essays, books, critics and theorists can enter the discourse. Is there a way to begin talking about value that does not automatically slot the discussion into that well-worn groove 'shaped by British and Austrian empiricists, German Kantians and neo-Kantians, American pragmatists and realists, and logical empiricists around the world'?[1] Can I talk about it without having to re-enact or work through the dialectic of absolute value and relative value as Connor does when he recommends 'the acceptance of the radical self-contradiction and unabatable paradox of value'?[2] If I can start at some place that refuses to accept the binary opposition of ethics and aesthetics and the many allotropes for these terms that Connor provides, then perhaps I will not have to attempt to outflank it at all, as Connor tries to. And to do this might feed back into the book's argument in the sense that perhaps there is another beginning that does not depend upon a continuing oscillation between structure and process, metaphysics and contingency.

One way would be to simply ask people what they think Literature, and the value of Literature, is. It is logical to assume that Literature exists in people's perception of it. But then, why choose that particular route, what would be the value of it? And then, what would I mean when I said value?

Well, we might begin by splitting value into three areas: use-value, exchange-value and pleasure-value: I cannot proceed without defining value. This circularity of argument is wholly indicative of the nature of the discussion on value. It is a very tough nut to crack, unless one concedes that there does indeed exist an absolute standard against which other values can be measured. In the arenas of 'life', 'economics' and 'humanity' these absolutes would be, respectively, 'God', 'gold' and 'good'. But the book accepts the basic premise of postmodern theorising that no such standards are available in any of these ways as commonly understood (as positive and essential forces), since any one would require a leap of faith.

Instead of approaching value head on, let us begin the chapter again, but tangentially, by way of the following question: Is there such a thing as a value-free fact? Are all facts implicated (or compromised) by the notion of value?

The first possible refutation might be a fact such as $E=mc^2$. Can there be any possible value inherent in such an equation which so simply states the relationship between mass and energy? Well, yes. Such an equation is one way of seeing the world that has value for one culture or cultures but not others, or might even have value for one person within a culture and not others. Does this mean that the 'fact' (or 'interpretation' – after all, we might define mathematical equations as metaphors, and why describe the world in terms of mass and energy anyway?) has value at all times? To someone who does not see the world in this way, either by virtue of the fact that they do not use equations (perhaps they believe in magic, although to another culture this very equation might be an instance of magic) or that they rely on a wholly different set of equations, it is of no value, or deemed to be of no value. But then, is it a fact? It might be. I could answer that in your world it is a fact which I am quite prepared to accept as true but which is of no value in the general scheme of things, for example, everything for me might be related to what I believe about God, in which case I might exclaim that Einstein's equation is wholly irrelevant. In other words, to be an important fact, the fact must have value. To be a valueless fact is to be irrelevant, unimportant. Let us say that facts are value-free (neutral) therefore only to the extent that they are trivial. If the statement is important to me then it must needs be a value judgement. Only when the fact is of no importance to me can it be a value-free fact.

This is all very well, but it doesn't take us much further. The nut of value is far from being cracked and I remain in the position of waiting for God to come down and adjudicate, or of accepting (and then celebrating or despairing) at the infinite regress of value.

Let me start again. Can I say that Literature is a fact? I could say that 'Literature' is a metaphor for a set of relations and that, like $E=mc^2$, it has an aptness of fit, and also like Einstein's equation and any other metaphor, it is not the thing itself. Processes and structures behave and seem 'as if' they were Literature.

So imagine that we begin by stating that there exists something called Literature, and that we study this object. According to the reasoning above the fact comes to us value-laden (it is important enough to study). Before going any further there is an objection to this. For example, it might be argued that Literature as a concept is important but nevertheless Literature does not exist (similarly – God is important as a concept but does not exist). This is not sustainable as an objection since the Literature versus no-Literature argument (which is predicated upon the possibility that Literature exists, whether it does or does not) is important. So, *for the present*, we can state that the concept 'Literature' is important (for those who participate in it, use it, debate it, etc.), or as Anthony Appiah might put it, 'holds our interest'.[3] That Literature exists as a mode of discourse is therefore a fact. But this seems like a large hammer to crack a small nut, and it still remains the case that what constitutes Literature remains open to debate. Nothing has been cracked.

Let us make another tangential move and look at the value of Literature negatively through Tony Bennett's book *Outside Literature*, which makes a full-scale attempt to rethink the whole notion of Literature, approaching it from a sociohistorical perspective.[4] He looks at the question of aesthetics and argues in some detail against the construction of any theory based upon the notion of the aesthetic, or, indeed, any notion that Literature is intrinsically a special mode of writing, an argument in effect against giving Literature any special value of this order. As such, Bennett's book, as well as a means with which to approach value also provides a very useful platform from which to examine the problems of attempting to mediate between immanence-based theories of Literature and sociohistorical theories of Literature.

Bennett positions himself in a post-Marxist space. This entails a rejection of many of the central Marxist tenets: reality prior to ideology; being prior to consciousness; a unifying cause (class struggle); a teleological narrative (communism). Much of this is consistent with an acknowledgement and acceptance of the force of arguments within poststructuralism and postmodernism. For example, Bennett argues in the postmodern vein when he claims that metanarratives can no longer be granted any genuine force. He therefore rejects the possibility that there might be one all-encompassing theory. Obviously, the particular metanarrative Bennett eschews is Marxism. However, to counter the slide into relativism that this line of reasoning often yields, Bennett argues (much as Christopher Norris does in *What's Wrong With Postmodernism*)[5] that the free-play argument usually associated with deconstruction is the weaker of its arguments. This argument rests on the notion that truth should always be absolute, a tenet that is unsustainable according to this version of deconstruction. The natural consequence is that if truth is *not* absolute then the alternative must be that 'anything goes'. The stronger argument which deconstruction makes available, and which both Bennett and Norris favour, undoes the very polarisation that makes truth an absolute concept. Although *The Direction of Literary Theory* has been proceeding according to the 'stronger' version of deconstructive thinking, as stated in the Introduction (what is plausible rather than what is absolute), it remains the case that if we accept this 'stronger' *cultural* conceptualisation it enables us little more than the 'weaker' argument does, in that 'meaning' and 'truth' are arrested ('fixed') by the discourse ('culture') within which they operate. Rather than abstract (theoretical) relativism, the so-called stronger argument does little more than translate its relativism into the practical world of pluralism – in other words, at a theoretical level deconstructive thinking (postmodern theory) logically results in what can only be described as an absolute relativism, but the contingent forces of our day-to-day world always place limits on this absolutism and force a plurality of temporary, essentialist positions, with boundaries ineluctably set by such things as value and ethics.

To return to Bennett, his positioning at all points is one that views all elements involved in this kind of discourse (truth, text, history) as operating within socially-determined constructs, or rather, a system of social regulatory practices. This is his mediation between old totalising theories and new relativist trends. It also means he can maintain a socialist stance whilst at the same time jettisoning the old Marxist baggage. What is also necessary for Bennett is that the idea of 'Literature' as a *special* practice be abandoned, and that it be regarded simply as a *particular* practice, alongside, say, the history of law.[6] For Bennett, Literature has been taken as 'special' because of its supposed aesthetic nature. Connected with the notion of the aesthetic are the corollaries of the transcendental and the idealist, terms which according to Bennett should also be abandoned. As Bennett argues, it was inimical to Marxist epistemology that Marxist critical theory should work within the bourgeois concept of the 'aesthetic'. Hence Bennett believes that along with those aesthetic/idealist/transcendental terms, the entire epistemology that supported them should be rejected, something that can be achieved by concentrating on history and social practices. Drawing upon the work of Foucault and John Frow, the implication of the latter's contentions

> is that literary texts should be examined not to reveal what they say about past social relations but, through what they say, what they do within them where that doing is conditioned by the particular organisation and social placement of the literary formations which regulate the concrete forms of the social deployment and functioning of literary texts.[7]

To take Bennett's argument on its own terms, it seems contradictory that whilst insisting on the social network of relations and the text's deployment within that, he can discard 'the aesthetic' so categorically. On his own terms he would have to accept the concept 'aesthetic' as an essential part of the nexus he sets forth for the analysis of texts (which is one of the strengths of Hunter's Foucauldian approach). Even if he removes the aesthetic from the theoretical sphere he must acknowledge that it functions in a very real sense in 'the social deployment and functioning of literary texts'. Bennett's error is two-fold. Firstly is his notion of aesthetic philosophy. This is coloured by its use and appropriation by Marxist critical theory, which leads to his presumption that discussion of the aesthetic at all levels, from individual texts to Literature, seeks the transcendental in some idealistic way. Yet surely it is feasible to say that the *category* of 'the aesthetic' *is* 'transhistorical' in the sense that as a concept it goes beyond the local level of texts and operates at the macro level of our understanding, and that the aesthetic is constitutive of art in general and not just Literature (in the sense that it informs our understanding of the artistic intention as previously outlined), but that we do not necessarily need to argue that individual works of art embody a transcendental aesthetic quality. And at this point there is no need to decide whether this aesthetic is considered as being immanent in the work or a mode of understanding in relation to the reader-response approach. The important point is that the aesthetic is present in some form at all times when talking about Literature, since the aesthetic function is recognised as constitutive of the artistic intention (necessary but not sufficient). Bennett's argument against this is that all Literature is institutionally defined. But this is not necessarily an argument against the aesthetic, since surely Bennett can accommodate the 'aesthetic function' as a mode that is likewise socially and historically determined. It is his own description of the aesthetic, in terms that rely solely upon the Marxist interpretation and inheritance of the term, that prevent him from putting it into the social and historical nexus he demands. Bennett, by 'severing the aesthetic', is abandoning one of the most important elements – in the social and historical sense – that inform an understanding of Literature. According to Bennett, the removal of the aesthetic connection does not necessarily entail the abandonment of the category 'Literature'.[8] Yet it is hard to see why he should insist that the 'connection' should be 'severed'. It is his use of metaphor, 'linking' 'spheres', which allows this rather specious manoeuvre, rather than regarding the aesthetic function – either as immanent or as part of the social and historical deployment of texts – as in some way integral to Literature. If Literature is a specific mode of a practice of writing, integral to that is the production of the aesthetic (or a working within the aesthetic), it is constitutive of that practice without having to exhibit the transcendence (in terms of being outside history and society) that Bennett clearly finds the most distressing part of it. It is simply necessary to look at the work of Jan Mukarovsky and the Prague Linguistic School to see that not all those theoreticians who work with the category of the aesthetic take it as read that this involves transcendence. Mukarovsky's insistence that at all times the work of art is a sign, and therefore socially determined, argues that the aesthetic function must also therefore be socially determined and subject to the passage of time, as well as subject to difference between cultures.

There are other objections to Bennett's argumentative framework. At exactly which points are we to view 'what they [literary texts] say' (see quotation above)? Given the absence of any possibility of 'fixing' (a representation of) society, since there is now (Bennett draws upon Lacow and Mouffe) no object of study that can be called 'society', how can there be anything other than an indefinable amorphous mass of interrelations that are changing, not just from century to century, but from minute to minute? To say anything about the use of texts Bennett would have to fix at some point a set of regulatory relations to determine (or determine at that time) the text's 'existence', 'set of meanings', whatever it is that Bennett is actually looking for. In the absence of concrete examples, it is impossible to know exactly what it is Bennett hopes to achieve when faced with a literary text, other than an arbitrary description of societal relations which coincide with what the text has to say. Alternatively perhaps Bennett's argument is that it is the deployment of the text that 'says' something, but it all seems hopelessly contradictory.

This leads to another objection. What exactly is being recorded? Meanings of texts throughout their reception history? In which case is this not Jauss's *Rezeptionaesthetik* (without the aesthetic!), looking at texts against 'the horizon of understanding'? Or how a particular text moved within a particular 'society' at a particular time according to its 'use'? And how is this to be determined? An amalgamation of reviews, letters, critical articles? (And how would the aesthetic be regarded here?) But would this tell us anything of its 'use' by people *not* involved in these particular 'literary' formations? And couldn't 'use' ('deployment') in any case be a function primarily of 'the aesthetic', that literary texts are deployed according to their aesthetic value, a value that is *not* transcendental, to be sure, but that is socially determined and prioritised?

Tony Bennett takes it for granted, or the implication is there, that literary criticism can only be literary history, that it can only be understood as such. What would happen, I wonder, if Tony Bennett were to be presented with a newly published work? Would he have to wait for history to overtake it before he could pass comment? What could he say that was not just his version of societal dynamics of that day? Not that this is necessarily irrelevant, but just how significant would it be? Or is he only interested in Literature as a macro-concept that cannot address any individual item within that historical overview? Nor is there any room in Tony Bennett's schema for individual response – the presupposition must be that the self does not exist, but is a site of societal forces that precondition possible responses. And in this case would he be saying that 'the aesthetic' category did not exist anywhere at all?

Outside Literature also tackles the issue of pedagogy, treating it very much as the point of arrival for his arguments on 'aesthetics' in part three and 'the role of the literary intellectual' in part four. Given the criticism he makes of 'Literature', as he understands it – that is, as a mode of deployment of texts within institutions, institutions which serve to inscribe values of elitism, especially in their use of 'depth' metaphors where only those readers with the correct institutional and institutionalised knowledge will 'understand' Literature – he demands a demystification of these practices which have elevated the aesthetic. For as Bennett sees it: 'Reading aesthetically, therefore, is not a matter of recognising the text's objective literary and aesthetic properties but a matter of behaving correctly within a particular normative regime of reading.'[9] From this standpoint he goes on to state just how Literature in education might continue. He suggests that rather than subscribing to a *way* of reading, (that is, that appears to be ethically/politically oriented and in which there are no *correct* readings – the modern critical approach), he argues for

> the emergence of a more progressive literary pedagogy and criticism. One possibility, for example, might consist in the development of exercises, tests, and forms of assessment through which readings can be assessed as definitely correct or not in relation to stated (and hence debatable) criteria, thus constituting the teacher/critic as a technical rather than, say, an ethical exemplar and involving the student/reader in the acquisition of particular technical competencies rather than in an unending process of ethical self-correction.[10]

This to me begs the question of just what level in the education system Bennett is criticising? Does he take this 'unending process of ethical self-correction' to be rife all the way through from primary to higher education? He seems to have conflated what are in essence two separate criticisms. The first might be applied to pre-higher education (GCSE and A-level in Britain) and refers to the question of aesthetics and its ethical constitution, where perhaps it could be argued that 'a normative reading process' takes place (although I would regard even this as highly debatable). The second relates to a number of different ways of reading or approaching texts, with no single 'correct' reading to be expected. This latter is surely applicable to teaching at degree level, where there is a range of critical approaches available that exist without the necessity for ethical correction or concern with aesthetics. In my experience assessment of student's work is usually dependent upon criteria of persuasive argument, and it would be churlish to say that 'persuasive' was only applicable when the student confirmed the ethical stance of the assessor.

However, to give Bennett's argument its due, let us imagine what his recipe for change might look like in practice. Immediately there is a double-bind. What text(s) am I to choose? Texts that have not been deployed within the institutions that constitute 'Literature' cannot logically be used because they are not yet Literature. This leaves me with one of two choices. I either accept a 'literary' text – which will by definition be canonical and 'Literature' – or I redefine what counts as 'Literature'. Yet this is a problem only if we take Bennett's assessment at face value. His argument is that 'Literature' is really an institutional process and structure that deploys texts for its own self-perpetuating ends, in other words, an ideological state apparatus. Presumably these necessary texts could or would be any texts that were available or open to the process and structure Bennett delineates. A cursory glance at Literature courses would surely be enough to convince that virtually anything can be studied under the rubric of 'Literature' that has a printed format. The onus is then on Bennett to define what texts *should* be used. This would no doubt be a consequence of what 'exercises, tests and forms of assessment' are selected. What kind of teaching could this possibly be that did not fall into either a study of grammar, with all its attendant problems of what linguistic theories and categories to use, or discourse analysis, but that would not eradicate problems of interpretation, which is really what Bennett strives to remove. What kind of exercises and tests could possibly be applied that did not involve interpretation and ideological presuppositions at some level? Would it not also depend on how this teaching described what 'the text' (at the conceptual level) consisted of – structures? issues? language? ideology? author's messages? – *before* it could even begin to ask questions of the text itself?

Bennett's call to arms demands criteria that allow for logical, rational and 'reasonable' discourse. The meaning of none of these terms is self-evident but rather open to negotiation, especially 'reasonable', and vulnerable in ways that would completely undermine the whole thrust of Bennett's book. In short, Bennett argues that the whole value of Literature as it currently stands and has stood for a long time is one of transcendence, ethics and aesthetics. Yet Bennett's argument is in itself based on a moral objection (whether right or wrong) along the lines of high/low Literature. How is *this* to be grounded in the postmodern environment that Bennett accepts? It can be nothing more than his own leap of faith into the post-Marxist (Karl who?) socialist space he believes has been cleared. Nor is it necessary to believe that aesthetics alone constitutes the special nature of Literature or is where its value lies (see Part II). Once again, the value of Literature, like the 'object' itself (if indeed it is an object) proves elusive, despite the concerted and quite persuasive attack provided by Bennett.

Another attack upon the special nature of Literature, that is, its perceived special value, and its pedagogical status, is provided by Antony Easthope. He attempts to dissolve literary studies into cultural studies, as the title *Literary into Cultural Studies* suggests.[11] Easthope, like Bennett, must obviously define his object of attack in a way which will not only suggest that the study of Literature is ripe for transformation but will also allow for its transformation. This is easily done by stating that Literature is a cultural product. Rather than simply doing away with it he argues for a different way of thinking, one which favours a reading of all culture (which for Easthope consists of films and adverts as well as books). I would here make the point I made with respect to Literature and history, that because there are similarities – with history it is narrative, here it is a belief that any cultural production is open to a sociohistorical reading – it does not entail an equivalence. As with Bennett, the main desire to completely overhaul Literature springs from the dislike for the position it appears to maintain as a discipline that reinstates high/low Literature and concomitant elitist values. We either do away with any notion of literary understanding other than that which can be scientifically or objectively assessed (Bennett) or we say that novels, poetry and drama are no different from soup can labels (Easthope).

Let us take the soup can label argument. It might be said that, and this is both Bennett's and Easthope's argument in essence, no doubt part-derived from poststructuralist thinking, that a text is a text is a text, and to argue differently is to accord a status to Literature (or to invent the whole notion of Literature) whose foundation is one of a detestable (elitist) ethics. For them Literature is no different from any other writing: it consists of texts. Well, yes, to study a soup can label can tell the observer many things – if looked at in certain ways. If the observer asks what it may say about advertising processes, food consumption, social make-up, it may be useful (or whatever evaluative criteria they feel is at issue – pleasure, exchange, etc.). If the questions are of the order of what it can tell us about the existence of charmed quarks or the shoe-industry its value is negligible. To study or to view Literature in the same way as a soup can label is to permit certain questions only because of the presuppositions, it is to attend to certain factors.

But why not regard the soup can label as Literature too? To take the argument on its own terms, we can, but we are either going to say that it is uninteresting, say, linguistically or aesthetically, or not very good. We will not be able to say very much about it at all if looked at through the lens of Literature. In other words, to ask questions about Literature through the lens of, say, sociological theory, is to regard Literature as a sociological phenomenon. This would, of course, lead to the same problems experienced by the book so far – What is society? What constitutes it? And similarly 'Cultural Studies' presupposes an entity called 'culture'. Why should this be considered to exist and Literature not, or exist as a preferable (hypothetical) entity? Certain objects require certain lenses, or are better seen through certain lenses: I cannot see an amoeba with the unaided naked eye. The discourses of aesthetics and ethics allow us to say many things about certain objects, and as we look through these lenses must part constitute the subject and object. The value inheres to the relationship between lens and object.

But once again I appear to be using a very large hammer to crack or defend what seems self-evident, the study of Literature and the study of soup can labels (cultural semiotics, let us say) are not coterminous at all points. Let us make the nut bigger.

There is something called Literature which involves something called literary understanding. Literary understanding is not a separate entity or process, it is a necessary condition of the existence of Literature. The two things imply each other. But what is this literary understanding if not some elitist constant utilised to cower the masses into moral submission, to accept the mores of the bourgeoisie (which is what Bennett and Easthope are really objecting to)? The argument against Literature as it is perceived to stand by Bennett and Easthope is that it is a function of its history (which is taken to be its material foundation). In other words, being materialists *par excellence*, (although in the post-Marxist space they inhabit can a 'materialist' programme have an *a priori* rationale such as 'the material'?), they define Literature etymologically. Of course, the problem with that is the same as trying to define a word as it is used now by referring to its history. A word is not defined by an earlier usage (from, say, two millennia ago), but by its place within the current scheme of language, (obviously the structuralism argument). In other words, to know what Literature once was (if it was this moral tool) – and presumably Easthope and Bennett have in mind solely English studies, a fact which also damages their argument – does not mean we have a description of how it functions now. Secondly, their descriptions presuppose singular historical interpretations where their telos (the final point-of-view) determines their narrative. The final point-of-view, to which they narrate and which perforce must structure their narrative, is their synchronic assessment of how (the study of) English Literature now stands within institutions, and all this is to be done using a non-Marxist socialist paradigm of history (if that is possible – will 'class' be a tool of analysis, or does this too fly out the window along with Marxism?). This means in effect that they use a diachronic methodology to explain a synchronic phenomenon. It may be the case that the value of Literature, literary studies and literary understanding might be determined historically, but once again there is no definitive way of proceeding, since there are a number of teloses to choose from and no way of deciding from first principles which would be the correct one, or even which would be a better principle: the class struggle? *a* class struggle? the exclusion of women? the values of humanism? the value given to English Literature by first-year undergraduates?

One major problem with the argument thus far in the chapter is that it has maintained the fact-value dichotomy at some level, another version of the two camp scenario. Theorists as philosophically far apart as Barbara Herrnstein Smith[12] and Alasdair MacIntyre[13] challenge such a duality, as does John Fekete in his essay 'Vampire Value'.[14] The latter suggests a programme that holds out the hope of reconceiving the problem of value. He describes the old way of thinking in this manner:

Representational models have accustomed us to taking for granted a picture of value as a derivative or metonymic property, with the result that we speak routinely of the semantic value of a word, the time value of a note in music, the quantity of an algebraical term, or the equivalent that may be substituted for a commodity. Evaluation, accordingly, comes to be understood as a procedure to provide the comparative measure of such representations.[15]

Against this Fekete recommends a programme that could develop value 'as a move to displace the commodity conception of value and to advance a picture of value as the regulative medium of preference'. It is clear that such a manoeuvre would crack the fact-value problem because it is simply saying that whatever we do, say, or think, is always under the sway of the process of evaluation, that is, we prefer some things to others. We might see it as a change from a classical system where items have an innate, positive value, to a system described in a structuralist vein where the value of an item is relative to other items within the same system. In this new system value becomes purely a process (economy) of differentiation and not the metonymic sign for something else. In the old system, the metonymic chain was arrested only at some absolute such as God, good or gold. However, this amounts to little more than a changeover in nomenclature, as can be seen if we try to put Fekete's argument into Literature.

In the old way of looking at things, value was preordained and absolute, for example, we might have said '*Hamlet* is one of the best plays in the world'. In the new programme, value is purely the name of the regulating process of the economy, it is the mechanism of the economy of Literature where we happen to prefer *Hamlet* to lots of other plays, not because there is something essentially great about it, but according to whatever criteria the economy provides at that particular time. At this point Literature is therefore being defined by Fekete as a system of distribution, reception, exchange and negotiation which does, or does not, keep *Hamlet* in circulation. Fekete's agenda suggests that the value of *Hamlet*[16] is now deemed to be contingent upon the economy it finds itself in, although presumably this is not necessarily a market economy, since *Hamlet* might be kept in circulation for 'cultural' reasons, it is just that there is an 'economy' in operation. *Hamlet* thus is now described as existing purely within the process of evaluation, whereas previously it fitted into some Great Chain of Value. Fekete has in effect re-enacted the absolute/relative value dialectic to come down firmly on the second, pragmatist term, where value is always there without regard to a foundational epistemology or ontology, where value does nothing more than exist by virtue of the functioning of a system, an economy, known as 'evaluation'. There is certainly a whiff of tautological reasoning in all this. Later in the chapter we will see how Fekete switches back over to the other side, to the side of absolute value.

Still, none of this automatically invalidates the possible advantages of seeing Literature in terms of an economy and striving to crack the value-nut in that way. Nor does it immediately invalidate the possibilities of Fekete's programme. He does, however, run into problems as soon as he applies his scheme of economic process in more detail, illustrating that he is far from breaking the absolute/relative nut:

> the regulation of the distribution and reception of literature is arguably far more powerfully instituted than would seem to be the regulation of literary creation. As a general consequence, a theory of literature and literary value cannot be narrowly identified with a theory of evaluation from the perspective of reception; that is, a theory of literature must be more and other than a theory of literary criticism, if it wants to take in the entire circuit of literary value.[17]

'Regulation of literary creation'? On the most general level this poses, or should pose, no problems – an economy involves production/creation as well as reception/consumption. It is difficult to understand why in fact the regulation of literary creation/production should provide a stumbling block since in an economy production is linked to consumption, usually quite intimately. The degree of influence will obviously depend upon which economic model underwrites the metaphor, and as an aside, it might be that the prevalence of 'exchange' and other economic terms in literary theory and criticism, notably New Historicism, is a consequence of the obsession with 'the market' which was so noticeable in the 1980s, epitomised in Martin Amis's *Money* and the film *Wall Street*. The reason literary creation does provide a difficulty is because, when it comes to the crunch, Fekete himself wants to claim a positive, essential, innate, transcendental value for art, in effect a reversion to the Classical system. For Fekete the value of art turns out to be a claim on his part that there is an autonomous discourse within art which can be described as the questioning of the value of value,[18] something which in turn can underwrite literary creation *independently* of its reception. This clearly undermines Fekete's argument since the 'questioning of the value of value' is an absolute term and not itself subject to the question of evaluation – that is, it does not suffer the fate of the question 'what is the value of questioning the value of value?' etc. – the spectre of infinite regress is therefore exorcised by this absolute definition of the aesthetic. Otherwise, unwittingly, in Fekete's scheme, once the concept 'art' comes under any process of evaluation, it (art) is made valueless because it is rendered non-autonomous, that is, it becomes dependent for its 'value' on criteria that are extrinsic to it. Fekete cannot provide a meta-evaluative process. Such a process might have to be pre-determined anthropologically, that is, art along with its creation and appreciation, would have to be taken as an anthropological universal given, a fundamental fact of existence (Ur-value) which would avoid the necessity to evaluate since it would be, indubitably, a fact of (pragmatic) existence. Given Fekete's outline of the new system of evaluation, however, such a solution is not possible.

Part of the problem for Fekete here, I would suggest, is that the economy known as 'Literature' remains undefined. Yet this in itself should be a simple case of determining the rules of regulation with regard to evaluation, which would then tell us what exactly it was that was being regulated (that is, Literature). But even here there would be a problem in that regulatory parameters have shifted over the past six or seven decades so as to make the economy of Literature unrecognisable, that is, is it the same economy? How did evaluation, the system regulating Literature, as value does all economies according to Fekete, transform itself into a different evaluative system? What regulates the regulator? The difficulty is that value as conceived of by Fekete is a dynamic system *in equilibrium*, self-enclosed, self-regulating. It cannot, by itself, give the value, in the old sense, of its value (in both senses). So Fekete, as noted, has to turn to aesthetics in order to circumvent the consequences of the 'economy' metaphor, a metaphor which reduces the value (in the old sense) of literary creation. Instead he must give 'art' and the activity of art an absolute value. For Fekete, art is too valuable to be left to an economy that does nothing but regulate taste. This is how Fekete wields the hammer of aesthetic value:

> ... I am arguing that aesthetic value is not a consequence of some *particular* everyday interest, nor even a utility *sui generis* within the same continuum as the particular everyday sources of interest and value. Instead, aesthetic value may be intelligible as the name for a significant reflexivity of value: aesthetic value may be described as a force-field of value most prominently polarised around a special type of objectification (art) whose dynamics permit and demand the recoiling of value upon itself. Art may therefore be regarded as a site of a reflexive organisation of perceptual, rational, affective, and imaginary elements, all in terms of value.[19]

Aesthetic value is therefore the place where the value of value is questioned. This assertion on Fekete's part evades the issue of value by setting it at one further remove, and art is thus deemed a variety of reflexive exercises on the value of value. What began as the nut of value now becomes the nut of art. Nothing has been elucidated.

Let us look at value from the point of view provided by Steven Connor.

> Value ... is the irreducible orientation towards the better, and revulsion from the worse ... the irreducible principle of generalized positivity, the inescapable pressure to identify and identify with whatever is valuable rather than what is not valuable.[20]

How might this universal imperative work in practice? It is difficult to comprehend how the statement could have any application. It is one thing to say value and evaluation are everywhere (which at first glance seems true), but impossible to see how such a conception is in itself useful (or do I mean valuable?). There are similarities with Barbara Herrnstein Smith's musings over Shakespeare's *Sonnets* in her *Contingencies of Value*, which, although illustrating perfectly well one person's (her own) changing taste or evaluation of a particular set of texts, a vacillation which in itself mirrors the changing fortunes of esteem that the texts themselves have attracted throughout their history, we are left with little more than the fact that all value is contingent. The limit to both such approaches setting off with these axioms is provided by the response to a question I once asked some first year English undergraduates:

Q. 'What is the value of studying English Literature?'
A. 'What is the value of studying anything?'

To any question involving value it is clear, as illustrated at the start and in our assessment of Fekete, that we can come back and ask 'And what is the value of that?' The upper limit of this is 'What is the value of living?' Answer that and we can answer all the other questions that lead inexorably to it, and here again the answer will be of the God–Good–Gold variety. If the exploration of value cannot begin with providing the, or even 'a', universal that would anchor any such project, it is doomed to failure. Connor's project is underwritten, like many others since the 1960s (and especially in these politically correct times), by the absolute standard of 'freedom': 'The desirability of universal freedom may seem hard to dispute, but universal freedom (like universal anything) must include within it the freedom to question and criticize its own nature.'[21] Whilst few will query the sentiment, this raises a couple of questions. Is the kind of existential, Nietzschean freedom in Camus's *The Outsider* or Dostoevsky's *Crime and Punishment* universally desirable? And if we are to be theoretically consistent we must also force ourselves to ask why we should choose 'freedom' as an Ur-value, as our anthropological universal given? Connor's move is to argue for a 'thinking together' of relative and absolute value,[22] which certainly suggests a resolution for our two-camp scenario, although it is also hard to see how this is not some kind of 'doublethink'. It may be that such an escalation, from the question of value to the issue of totalitarianism and its related activities, is off the mark – yet such ethical questions are precisely at the back of both Smith's and Connor's tussles with evaluation. Connor picks up on Smith's discussion of 'how would you (as the relativist) answer the Nazi?'. Smith replies *'it depends'*.[23] Connor argues that this narrows the force of the question, 'which surely means not only "how would you be likely to answer the Nazi?" but how *should* you answer the Nazi?'.[24] The cases of both de Man and Heidegger are no doubt lurking. The universal drive toward the better is here being understood as an ethical drive, it valorises the ethical, and so the wedge between aesthetic value and ethical value remains firmly in place and problematical.

For the moment, then, neither the nature of facts nor 'the imperative toward what is better' can afford us any leverage, since any attempt to apply thinking on evaluation in general to Literature always leads us back to question the axioms of value, themselves (apparently) never far removed from questions of ethics. The question of value (like the question of interpretation) might therefore be better approached *after* the ethical framework has been elucidated. As it stands, to describe what value is is not to say what we can do with it. We are *in* value, just as we are *in* interpretation if we begin the problems in this way. To point out these difficulties cannot help acts of evaluation, cannot even begin to help approach value in Literature.

I would like to explore another way of looking at value and Literature which emerges from a book devoted to the project of providing such a new ethical framework, Alasdair MacIntyre's *After Virtue*.[25] MacIntyre's argument runs something along the lines that the modern moral crisis he identifies is a result of the collapse of the environment that would support (and, according to MacIntyre, did support at the time of Aristotle) such concepts as 'justice' and 'equality', a time when beliefs amounted to facts and could not be separated out. Barbara Herrnstein Smith convincingly criticises MacIntyre's own version of this Fall from virtue(s). However, part of MacIntyre's argument consists of the notion of 'telling stories' as a fundamental part and constitution of human existence. It is not the case that narratives are foisted upon past events, as Louis Mink and Hayden White have argued, which thereby only succeed in distorting the truth of those events, but that stories and events are mutually dependent and interwoven. To have one is to have the other, rather than having events which are autonomous and prior to the disfiguring, structuring narrative. Now imagine that we apply some version of this to the problem of value, interpretation (perhaps) and Literature. Or imagine that instead of using 'theory' to justify or explain what those involved in Literature are doing, or what their attitude and approach to it is (or mine is for that matter) we are really involved in telling stories. Now imagine that we have been telling ourselves, or have been told, the wrong story, and have placed ourselves (or been placed) in the wrong historical narrative.

In which story is it that value becomes 'exiled', as Barbara Herrnstein Smith (and Steven Connor and others concur) puts it? It is in the story of theory that traces Literary Studies (note *not* 'Literature') from Russian Formalism, through structuralism and poststructuralism, the latter now shading into postmodern theory (including New Historicism). Value may not, or does not, become exiled if we take either the view that this is the wrong story of theory, or that this story is only a minor plot in a more comprehensive story of literary study or Literature. Another story might proceed along the lines of the sketch whereby the history of theory is imbedded in the practice of Literature and literary study, and has been appropriate only in the terms of that praxis, instead of its own methodological rules and regulations. Rather than envisage the story of Literature in terms of how it has progressed through the eyes of theory, now culminating in a self-awakening which we call postmodern theory (which recognises contingency, resistance to closure – although of course this is my depiction of that story – and an acknowledgement of the tough nut of value), we can turn round and say that in the story of Literature in general, in education, the media, everyday-speak, value has always been there in its many forms, and *not* solely as a consequence of the high/low culture divide. It has only been exiled in theory, or a certain narrative of theory. In this story, then, theory has not been successful, it has finally been brought to heel by the exigencies of the story to which it finds itself subordinated. Another way of looking at it would be to say that theory does not have the authority to continually revise what it thinks Literature is or isn't. But does this alter what theory says (and can say) about value?

Well, it would now appear that the limits of theory are value and evaluation and, as seen in both this chapter, via Connor and Smith, and the last chapter, the ethical. A consequence is that theory is not a meta-discourse within and upon Literature and should not even think of itself as such. In fact, literary theory's major failing may be in not accepting its circumscribed position, and finding itself having to make exaggerated claims to gain status. I am not saying here, Fish or Knapp and Michaels style, that theory does not have consequences, it does, but these are always circumscribed by the story of which it is a subplot, or even subtext. The value of theory has therefore always been related to the value of Literature, however defined. Theory's reawakening to evaluation in this story is thus simply the beginning of its realisation that it is surrounded by – rather than itself surrounding – Literature and the value thereof and therein. Value is not the problem when talking about Literature that the theoretical study of value would have us believe or presuppose. But what is this value from within which we work?

The main response to the question I alluded to above, 'what is the value of studying English Literature?', was that it broadens the mind with respect to the world and life. This I think provides the larger narrative framework with which to contextualise theory. Anyone who has taught Literature I am sure will agree that this is the general attitude of students, whether such tutors or lecturers agree that this should be the case or not. Of course, there is nothing to prevent an attempt to alter the narrative drift of Literature, to say that 'theory' should not be the value that informs the telos rather than the value of 'mind-broadening' (although the two are not necessarily mutually exclusive). This only serves to point up the fact that it is a question of ethics, in the sense of 'ought', rather than any objective quality or factor. The question of how the starting-point for Literature might be reconceived in the light of value, and the evident limitations of theory as shown in this part (see the following concluding comments as well), provides the impetus for Part II.

CONCLUDING COMMENTS

The book so far provides a synchronic assessment of the state of theory within Literature. It has answered the attack of theory on such old-fashioned items as 'author', 'intention', 'literary' texts and 'value' in a number of different ways, and has shown that both sociohistorical and immanence-based theories fail to eradicate – either logically or empirically – these areas of interest. But to argue *against* is not necessarily to argue *for* anything in particular. It is no use pretending that simply by answering these criticisms and theories of Literature, and the study and understanding of it, Literature is untouched and restored to some previous, less problematic, understanding. It is not simply the case that because none of the theories holds up, from Wimsatt and Beardsley onwards, we can return to the pre-New Critical days when we (supposedly) 'just read books'. Part II in contrast to this part argues positively. It takes the view that we *cannot* proceed from theory as such (or work entirely within it) to solve the theoretical impasse between the theoretical camps – and although other reasons are given for this point of view in the next part, the very failure of all the preceding theories to achieve any lasting force or recognition, again either on an empirical level or a logically sustainable one – is evidence that theory cannot in itself be a starting-point. Also it should be said that the initial guiding force of the argument, as *originally* conceived, needs to be overhauled. It cannot be claimed that a mediation has been found between the two camps and their various manifestations as witnessed in the preceding chapters. I would identify two reasons.

Firstly, I still believe it true that theories, self-consistent approaches and methodologies, fall into one or other of these two camps, and that this tension, as Ray points out (and, as has been seen, most others) has been constant throughout theoretical discourse upon Literature, and remains so. However, the preceding chapters show that no theory in either camp can work without undermining its claim either on the one hand to be exclusively a theory of immanence, or on the other hand to be dealing exclusively with sociohistorical factors. In that sense, mediation is already there. But then, if the theories are self-contradictory on logical grounds, they are hardly theories, but approaches or methods (and even to call them 'methods', with its connotation of system, might be stretching a point). Mediation, in this light, is there as a practical consequence and practical exigency. We might also note this is the differentiation between strong and weak deconstructive positions.

Secondly, theory's own (implicit) story of itself in Literature is a self-aggrandising narrative that is incommensurate with Literature, unless we are prepared to accept that Literature is purely and simply the theorisation of itself. I would also add that at every turn we have seen the implicit underwriting of projects by ethical concerns that are extraneous to the theoretical argumentation. This criticism too forms the background to Part II.

Part II

6
Thanks for the Theory

So far *The Direction of Literary Theory* has tackled the issue of how to bridge the gap between immanence-based theories and socio-historical theories, the initial point from which the argument began. There was a belief that something along the lines of a synthesis, even a permanent interchange, could be the outcome of such a project. The previous chapters have worked from within the relationship between these two apparently mutually exclusive doctrines. With respect to the topics chosen – 'intention', 'value', 'postmodernism and history' etc. – it has become clear that any particular one will always involve at some stage engaging with some other. They are inextricably interlinked: this is the nature of the discourse. It has also become apparent that no matter which route is taken the initial project so conceived is unresolvable, except, theoretically, as some kind of 'doublethink'. It has also been constantly suggested that the main difficulty lay in how Literature was perceived in the first instance, since the starting-point would always predetermine the limits of what could be claimed. The book thus far has done its utmost to suspend judgement or definition of this entity called Literature, apart from the belief that something as vague as artistic (literary) intention (no matter where located) is a prerequisite to discuss Literature (Art). The result has been a series of assertions that are perhaps inevitable as soon as the initial premises are worked through (once again the initial point determines the outcome). A brief summary of the life work and thought of Jan Mukarovsky would serve as an example at this juncture.

Beginning as a structuralist and with notions that structures are concretised (as proposed in the philosophy of Phenomenology), and so always aware of the mutability of taste and judgement (hence the title of a collection of his essays, *Aesthetic Function, Norm and Value as Social Facts*;[1] inherent here are both structuralism and reader-response, prefiguring de Man's work), he sought, much as this project has done, to find a way out of the paradox that art 'objects' stay the same yet change from generation to generation. To deal with such contingency he eventually began to look for anthropological givens, that is, concepts that are fundamental to our description of human existence. To help solve the paradox of contingency and transcendence he looked for some 'universal aesthetic value'. Without such a universal underpinning there can be no absolute grounding for 'structure', the shadow of 'taste' (contingency) will always fall across the vision of transcendence.

Like Mukarovsky, and this thinking is not just confined to theories based upon structure, I see no other way to think any literary (Arts) theory through. There will always be some dependency on a universal anthropological given that must underwrite the project. The history of literary theory that we present to ourselves is a version of this procession of thought. In fact, it is nothing more than an extended version of Mukarovsky's writings. Derrida's 'Structure, Sign and Play',[2] often taken to be the point of crossover from structuralism to poststructuralism, has in its title interchangeable terms with those of the Mukarovsky book, shifting from the left-hand term 'function' to the right-hand terms of Mukarovsky's contingent 'value' and Derrida's equally contingent 'play'. It seems to me that a constant to-ing and fro-ing between these notions is all that is possible when working theoretically *within* the dialectic of hermeneutics and aesthetics and the variations on the theme that have taken place so far.[3] Without an anthropological given which would make the whole notion of art universal (and to my knowledge there isn't one) we are left with culturally determined and culturally located systems, processes and validations; culturally determined and culturally located structures, norms, values, signs and play. It remains purely a question of interpretation within each culture whether art is to be regarded as transcendental, contingent or both. There is no way of deciding from some meta-art perspective since neither argument can claim ascendancy (back to the Good–God–Gold problem). The journey of such to-ing and fro-ing is interesting but it must be acknowledged that there can be no destination (although it may be better to travel than to arrive in this instance). To continue conceiving of the problem in terms of the dialectic as such is always to be confronted by the impasse of the initial polarisation. I am now going to suggest that the place of theory within the study of Literature and the claims it makes be reconsidered. The arguments here might also be extended to the Arts in general. Then I shall suggest how we might reconceive our relationship to Literature (this too can probably be extended to the Arts in general). At the same time as working through theory at the logical abstract level, I will also put it into the context of current teaching, since, as will become clear, the very existence of literary theory does not depend upon the force of its own arguments.

THEORY

Literary theory can be put into the following generalised context: with respect to the institutions where it is taught, specifically, higher education, it has gained a reasonable foothold, and we now expect to see it on Literature courses in one form or another. If my own experience at Leicester University is typical, and similar stories are to be heard elsewhere, teachers, tutors, lecturers, 'facilitators', tend to fall into one of two camps (we may as well continue to bifurcate – it makes it easier for the deconstructionists). There are those who are hostile to theory, and there are those who favour theory and believe that it allows no place for people who just want to read books in an old-fashioned, Leavisite way (although this really is far from 'innocent' reading). Proponents of theory rubbish the non-theorists for their naivete. The anti- and non-theorists on the other side maintain a defensive superiority along the lines that they know best anyway, that, no matter what the fancy jargon used, all anyone ever does is read books and that no theory, method or approach can contain or explicate this activity to any formalisable degree. The other part of the contextual equation is that students, in the main, do not like theory – it is often a way of thinking they are not used to and have probably done their best to avoid throughout their education (I realise that this assessment is focused on the English education system, but the consequences as discussed later may be more generally applicable). These students often find literary theory irrelevant to their enjoyment and understanding of Literature. My limited understanding of the current situation is that theory is going to have the status of a bad smell lingering in the study of Literature until it is given a different role from the one it presumes for itself and maintains.

Tony Pinkney has stated that the future of literary theory is linked to the status accorded to it by pedagogy: 'the future of literary theory has an unavoidable pedagogic dimension, involving a constant effort to make this difficult field of work accessible to undergraduate students; if we lose this battle, literary theory has no worthwhile future at all'.[4] This is not as pragmatically innocuous as it sounds, and for the following reason. Literary theory in general is premised upon the idea that it is an exercise in logic. Theories ground themselves and believe that certain consequences ensue from these groundings. This can be seen in Formalism, structuralism, Marxism, feminism (ignoring for the moment those tendencies toward mysticism, an issue dealt with later); even, I would argue, in poststructuralism, since this theory must itself posit some transcendental epistemological point of reference in order to argue that no grounding can possibly be sustained by other theories (it is a question of belief on Derrida's part that every structure can be deconstructed, in other words, it is an *interpretation* of the structurality of structure. Analogous is Kevin Hart's assessment that Derrida 'develops a transcendental argument that any discourse will contain the means to call its metaphysical claims into question').[5] Thus it can be seen that literary theory in general sets itself up in a pseudo-scientific mode. Yet it is obvious that none of these theories, often mutually incompatible, can be verified, proved or disproved in the way that a theory – such as the earth goes round the sun – is accepted according to the rules of the scientific community. There is no way to decide whether Formalism is right or whether Marxism is right. They are basically antithetical, yet are both taught as theories to explain the functioning of Literature. Yet, for anyone teaching theory who is not a hardened theorist, it is self-evident that we are dealing with approaches and not theories. Note that I am not even doing anything as sophisticated as deconstructing the ground that each theory rests upon. Nor does my argument depend upon some other theory, such as the neopragmatist notion that theories have no necessary consequences. I am simply pointing out that by no stretch of the imagination can these particular viewpoints with which we approach Literature be called theories. We expect theories to be demonstrably true or disprovable. If not that, then we at least expect a theory to fit into a framework which can decide which theory has the greater explanatory power, something that the study of Literature and literary theory most evidently can*not* do. We might even expect a theory, if it is to be treated as a theory, to predict the future behaviour of the material under description. Whilst this surely sounds absurd within the context of literary studies, it would hardly be news to those in the sciences.

Undoubtedly the interest and desire for theory within the study of Literature arises from a desire to place it on a scientific footing (see below for an assessment of the situation even if this premise is not granted. The outcome is the same). This is at best misconceived, at worst foolishness. Theory has its uses in the Arts, but the very fact that mutually exclusive theories can inhabit the same field of discourse *without any means of deciding between them*, or even the will to do so, is surely evidence that the status of theory within Literature (and the Arts) is simply not that of the sciences (see below also for a modified view of how theory might be viewed within the sciences). This is not to valorise one at the expense of the other, it is merely to acknowledge that the framework for theory is different within the discourse of the Arts. Nor is this the Knapp/Michaels argument of non-consequentiality. In fact, what they say is that theory does not necessarily have the consequences it claims for itself – which is not to say that there are no consequences. They are pointing out that theory and practice are discontinuous in the sense that there is no preordained cause-and-effect relationship. From a practical point of view, we could regard the discourse of literary theory as one that has a variable amount of influence on literary studies, but such a view completely undermines theory's own reasoning and rationale, and would leave it in no better state than any single non-theoretical commentary or musing that might be proffered and found to be persuasive.

To return to the difference in status for theory within the sciences and theory within the Arts: astronomy and physics can prove *to their own satisfaction* that the earth travels around the sun and not vice versa. That the earth goes round the sun is 'true' in scientific terms, and is at the expense of any theory which claims the sun goes round the earth. There is no equivalence for theory in Literature. For example, a theory which promotes 'literariness' as the criteria for Literature, as opposed to one which claims there is no objective criteria but only a set of cultural practices, cannot be said to be wrong or right in the same way as the sun/earth argument. Nor is it a question of appeal to a metadiscourse that could decide between the two. The discursive field that constitutes physics also validates whatever goes on within it at any given moment. It does not have to resort to some discourse on metaphysics. In other words, given that the question is whether the sun revolves around the earth or vice versa, within the field of astronomy it can be decided according to its own rationale. In this sense theory certainly cannot have consequences in Literature. It must be regarded in some other way. Before moving on to just how it might be viewed I would like to answer three possible objections that might be raised against my summarisation of theory within the Arts and science.

Objection 1

The first objection is that theory as used in the Arts, and particularly literary theory, does not have the same meaning or import as it does when considered in the sciences. This would be along the lines of saying that any theory within the Arts/Literature was more of an approach or methodology than theory. At a practical level, as mentioned in the introduction to the first part, this would certainly appear to be the case. Although the history of literary theory would show that as each theory has appeared it has claimed to be powerful in the way that a scientific theory is, in terms of explanatory force as well as in its ability to supplant all previous theories of Literature, no theory has proved capable of demonstrating itself to be the supreme one, though we have seen the predominance in certain institutions of single theoretical schools *as if* this were the case (Yale, for example). Since the problem is resolved at a practical level, with the cohabitation within the study of Literature of incompatible theories, it might seem that there is little more to say on the matter. Yet this situation is a blatant nonsense. Is one methodology or approach better than another? How are we to decide? If there are no hard-and-fast interpretations and analyses – semantically, aesthetically, evaluatively – with which we can test any particular approach as to its effectiveness we have not advanced one jot from the pre-Formalist days, since any judgement on the pertinence of any one methodology is purely a subjective judgement that cannot be subject to rational critique. There *is* a type of regulation in academia that passes itself off as objective evaluation when others' arguments are damned for being 'untheorised' – but this means only that a critic has not used some pre-ordained theoretical view-finder. It is not, as the charge suggests, that someone's argument falls down on logical grounds, and that logical grounds are available elsewhere, because clearly there *is* no logical grounding available elsewhere.

Another response to evaluating the efficacy of a theory has been to promote the idea that the more discourse any particular model generates the better it is – so such 'masters of discourse' (Foucault's terminology) as Freud, Marx and Saussure would evidently have the best theories. The difficulty with this – what amounts to a market-driven concept of the pragmatist's evaluative criteria – is that it reduces to an argument whereby those with power, the economic clout, or more directly, institutional clout, decide which models are to win out at any given time. Theory, methodology, literary theory: none of these can be said to be continuous with the claims they make for themselves, with respect to exhibiting demonstrable logic, since their efficacy is purely to be related to some economy outside of their own parameters and *not* their own reasoning power. It may be that as regards theory within the Arts and Literature this practical solution is the only available one, and that a calculation of the number of Modern Language Association (MLA) and Social Science Index citations is a ready indicator of the value of a theory. If this is to be the case, at least we should more openly admit the relativity, contingency and non-tenability of all theoretical discourse when we are expected to take it on its own terms. This is certainly not to say we are out of the quagmire of knowing what Literature is in that we can choose the most procreative theory, it is just to admit that there is an informal system which validates one or two theories at any given time. However, who would be prepared to support such a process as the agreed version of what would decide the best (if we are not to have logically coherent) theory? Even though many are prepared to acknowledge that the pressure *is* to publish and that this is meant to provide evidence of valuable critical activity, furthering the cause of knowledge, it is unlikely that anyone would actually subscribe to this process as a means of determining theoretical validity.

Objection 2

It can be argued that my portrayal of scientific endeavour does not take into account that in practical circumstances science itself does not actually possess the means suggested to decide between theories, that there are no hard-and-fast rules to decide between competing models. A current example might be the controversy surrounding James Lovelock's theory of the earth, known as Gaia, what he calls planetary medicine.[6] He claims that the earth exists in the manner of a living organism, that it is a sick patient with deteriorating lungs and poor circulation. The more common and scientifically accepted model of the earth is that it is a lump of rock with some water on top. Although Lovelock's approach is classified by many scientists as at best eccentric, their real antagonism may be that there *is* no way to decide between these competing metaphors, and that the scientific way is shown, when pushed, to be nothing more than a metaphor, even if it is the dominant one. Yet this objection to my delineation of theory within the sciences would be to deny those other areas in science where there is virtually no dissent – the discovery of the model for DNA for example. No such equivalent models can be said to operate within literary theory – even if the way deconstruction and Bakhtin's dialogism have been hailed and treated suggest otherwise.

A further objection is that theory within the sciences no longer claims to have the status presumed above, that it too, like postmodern theory in the Arts, acknowledges its own limits and contingencies. This might be explained cursorily by saying that the notions of 'chaos' have been taken on board by science. 'Chaos theory' states that there can never be enough information to understand and predict with complete (any) certainty any given system. It is tied up with the notion of non-linear systems: a very small change at the beginning of an event can have a drastic effect on the outcome ('chaos theory' is not therefore about 'disorder' as its name might suggest). There are two things to be said. Firstly, it is hardly taken as read that the greater part of the scientific community has been taken over by this 'paradigm shift' (the phrase that most popular expositions of the topic use, derived from Kuhn's *The Structure of Scientific Revolutions*),[7] rather, the practice of science has remained to a large extent unaffected by this theoretical paradigm, just as the reading of Literature outside academia has remained largely unaffected by the rise of literary theory over the past three or four decades.

Secondly, so what? If Literature is a system which eludes linearity (whatever that might entail) there is not a lot we can do, theoretically speaking. There appears little alternative but to relegate theory at this point and promote a philosophy of Literature as at least more honest, and open to judgement as such. If Literature does always elude systemisation how can we study it except under the influence of some desire? Are people interested in Literature because of theory? That would seem an absurdity. If theory is a discourse of its own, then Literature is likewise not beholden to it. We have come full circle, except that we have the knowledge that theory cannot be used on its own terms to circumscribe Literature. The circle is closed because we are still left asking just how can, or how should, Literature be viewed? This is linked to the third objection.

Objection 3

Whilst it might be granted that we cannot expect there to be a theory existing within and for Literature and the Arts that would have the force of 'the earth goes round the sun', we might have a theory of the type applied within physics to the nature of 'light'. Sometimes light behaves 'as if' it were a 'wave', and sometimes it behaves 'as if' it consisted of particles (photons), yet both cannot be true at the same time. For literary theory this might be treated as an acceptance that texts actually functioned, or could be viewed as operating, in the way that different theories claimed they did, but only under certain circumstances or within certain parameters.

This would overcome the problem of the mutual exclusiveness of sociohistorical (contextual) and immanence (textual) theories: sometimes texts behave as if they were 'authors' messages', sometimes as 'autonomous, self-sufficient constructs', sometimes as the manifestation of wider social concerns (it sounds convincing to me, yet is it any different from 'doublethink'?).

A further analogy might be that of the different forces science claims to be operating at different levels of analysis – at the macro-physical end of the scale are the gravitational forces that affect large bodies, and at the micro-physical end the nuclear forces operating at sub-atomic levels. This is analogous to the difference between much of the problem over the divide between sociohistorical and immanence theories. The latter are more applicable to purely textual matters at a particular and discrete level (deconstruction, 'close-reading'). However, the fact that it can only be said to be 'more applicable' is a sign that the analogy can only be pushed so far, since historical evidence can also explain small textual problems, such as the usage of a particular word. The fact that both science and the Arts use metaphors as models for explanation does not alter the fact that such a process in the sciences has a means of evaluating those models in terms of their aptness of fit, usefulness, elegance (economy) and predictability. In the Arts, in the teaching of theory, as already stated, which models are used is purely a question of current fashion, a tutor's individual preferences and politics.

Yet this third objection remains only within the discourse of theory, even if it does point a way out (by analogy) from the theoretical stalemate I have been exploring. It demonstrates once more that 'theory' within the Arts and Literature is dependent upon the status of theory within science and the principles said to be in force there. The arguments above in the third objection are using metaphors imported from science because theory within Literature and the Arts has no choice but to proceed as if it were a scientific tool for the attainment of knowledge, as opposed to other criteria we might use (and have used in the past) such as 'interesting' or 'fun' or 'beautiful' or 'clever', themselves surely as much drives as the desire for 'knowledge' within Literature.[8] To import the scientific environment as casually as literary theory does also leaves unanswered ideas of 'predictability' and 'verification' (Hirsch notwithstanding on the latter). To begin to contemplate the Arts and Literature under such concerns is to show the limits of theory for such ventures. What if Literature and the Arts are predicated primarily, inherently, implicitly, upon always outrunning our understanding and enjoyment of it, or predicated upon always outrunning our response to it? This is not the way of science, it proceeds along the lines of bringing within its remit and comprehension certain phenomena.[9] Physics *is* the study of physical phenomena. But Literature and the Arts are *not* constituted by the study of them. They are *human* creations. In this sense, and given that they cannot be subject to statistical laws, such things as 'philosophy' and 'ethics' *must* play their part. The following is an attempt to show what a non-foundational philosophy of Literature might look like.

A NOTE ON PHILOSOPHY AND MYSTICISM

It would possibly be more accurate to term what follows – if it did not carry such unacceptable connotations – mysticism. Mysticism has often been castigated as philosophy's 'other'. Kevin Hart notes that mysticism has been regarded 'as that which must at all costs be excluded from philosophical discourse'.[10] Indeed, Hart identifies this need for exclusion in the reception of deconstruction, as Spivak's framing of the debate in her introduction to Derrida's *Of Grammatology* illustrates:

> Speaking of the process of deconstruction, Spivak issues a stern warning to the reader: 'Let me add yet once again that this terrifying and exhilarating vertigo is not "mystical" or "theological"'. This is a curious moment in a text which has talked so animatedly about the danger of adding supplements.[11]

Further to this I would add (risking another dangerous supplement) Hart's following distinction between philosophy and mysticism as suggesting that mysticism would be nearer the mark as a description of any antifoundational philosophy:

> Yet if the borders of philosophy are continually expanding, it is nonetheless true that mysticism represents philosophy's

'other', a discourse (or at any rate, a family of discourses) concerned with truth and reality but which repudiates philosophical method and which prizes certain experiences over reason and language. Whereas philosophy licenses itself as prosecutor and judge, mysticism appears closed to dialectical inspection. The mystic's vision finds expression in metaphors, hyperboles, oxymorons, prosopoeia – in tropes of every kind – which are anathema to philosophical lucidity, and all the more alien to philosophy since the thought which gives rise to them seems anything but confused.[12]

If what has been said to date is true, and that nothing, either in theory or philosophy, has uncontestable and irrefutable grounds, then all theory and philosophy are in essence mysticism in any case (don't Derrida and other metaphysicians of his ilk actually *sound* like mystics?). However, to avoid Part II being automatically thrown out, I shall reaffirm that what follows is an attempt to begin a philosophical outlook as opposed to an overtly theoretical one.

7
Alterity: Martin Buber's 'I-Thou' in Literature and the Arts

It is obvious from the previous remarks that 'theory' is in no position to ground itself. From what we can observe of the movement of literary theory to grasp and elucidate Literature – and the fact that theory cannot ground itself does not imply it fails to address areas of importance for Literature – there has been a preoccupation with interpretation, aesthetics and ethics. A problem which currently plagues (or graces, depending upon your position) much theoretical and critical discourse is the notion of 'the Other', the problem of alterity.[1] Why should this be the case? It does not appear consistent with the arguments centred on the Literature-as-autonomous/Literature-as-sociohistorical phenomenon divide. Its appearance in postcolonial, feminist and sometimes postmodernist discourse (and the three are not always discrete) would suggest it favours the sociohistorical side of the divide, although a little more consideration might show its immanent, transcendental and ultimately mystical qualities (an issue we will return to). Its importance to feminist and postcolonial theory is self-evident. Its relation to more recent discussions on postmodernism is also obvious if we take Robert Young's description of postmodernism as 'European culture's awareness that it is no longer the unquestioned and dominant centre of the world'.[2] The huge influence of Bakhtin on recent literary theory in most areas also suggests the prevalence of the concern with alterity. The point is forcibly made by Iris M. Zavala:

> The question of *alterity* (*alterité, autrui*) is one of the vantage points of much poststructuralist linguistic theory, specifically decon-

struction and psychoanalysis. It is also the explicit focus of Bakhtinian theory of the sign and communicative systems, where communication and interpretation are seen to be dependent upon real or implied 'otherness', as co-participants in the 'event'. 'Voices', that is, 'semantic positions' are responsive, open to response; otherness refers to 'voice interferences' and the *dialogic*, as interlocution with 'others' (including readers) who must yet respond.

The Bakhtinian 'other' is the speaking individual as well as the speaking collective, the co-participant in an utterance.[3]

Also, given the influence of Derrida on much theory, it is not surprising that 'the Other' has surfaced, since he in turn is indebted to the work of Levinas where 'responsibility to the Other' exists 'pre-originally' and 'an-archically'.[4] This has proved most fortuitous in the desire to reintroduce ethics into theory at a time when political correctness is everything and when ethics had virtually been eliminated from the mainstream of theoretical debate, thanks to those very theories which would have done away with it, namely structuralism and poststructuralism; likewise the New Historicism that descends from Foucault, although not the New Historicist practice of Jerome McGann which Brook Thomas (as already stated) identifies as a separate strand[5] and the cultural materialism deriving from Raymond Williams. I would argue that the interest in 'the Other' is a consequence of the unacknowledged necessity of theory to ground itself in an anthropological universal given, since 'the Other' can certainly and rather simplistically be argued to be everywhere – something or someone always stands in opposition to something else or someone else somewhere along the line. The thinking is clearly dependent upon Saussurean/Derridean notions of binary oppositions. At present 'the Other' functions as the binary opposition to end all 'others'. If theory *could* make out the case that 'the Other' is here, there and everywhere (as it seems to), then what could be said about 'the Other' would hold good for *all* aspects of Literature (art, life, etc.). However, rather than proceed with the notion that 'the Other' can indeed provide the anthropological universal given that will solve all our theoretical problems (the book remains ever sceptical that this holy grail can be located) let me emphasise that what follows is not intended to be taken as a 'theory'. It is a 'philosophy' (and is really what all theories in the Arts should consider themselves as). What follows then, it should be reiterated, does not consider itself a 'theory' of Literature, but a philosophy that 'believes' Literature has certain properties and is dependent upon certain outlooks and predications.

The 'evidence' of the outbreak of 'the Other' in literary theoretical discourse across a number of areas is testimony to the saliency of such a discussion. However, to follow the previous chapter, this is certainly not to be taken as supporting a notion that 'the Other' provides one of the best theoretical models, simply that an analysis of it provides a pertinent ready-made starting-point. Allied to this there will be an assumption (a set of beliefs, 'a philosophy') on the part of *The Direction of Literary Theory* that literary theory fails 'to understand' (we would not use the word 'fails' if it accepted its own remit and parameters) Literature because there is always a disjunction between 'the reading experience' ('just reading books') and the (academic) discourse *about* Literature. The following is an attempt, therefore, both to elucidate the philosophy and to place 'the reading experience' into some kind of formulation that can enable us to talk about it. I would even suggest that the continual waverings between ethics and aesthetics, or hermeneutics and aesthetics, across all literary theories, might be taken as allotropes of this single element, just as coal and diamond are allotropes of carbon, and that this current concern with 'the Other' is a manifestation of an attempt to get to the underlying structure (other conceptual anchorings will no doubt supersede 'the Other'). To enable discussion along these lines I would like to turn to the book *Ich und Du* (*I and Thou*) by the Jewish philosopher Martin Buber, first published in 1923, as being germane to a number of *The Direction of Literary Theory*'s ongoing concerns by virtue of its suggestiveness. 'Suggestiveness' is used to make clear that neither the analysis of 'the Other' or 'Buber' is grounded in anything other than the wish to take part in current academic thinking, and that such analysis sheds further light on the function of theory, especially when it has to operate within the context of 'the Other', and the relationship between all parties concerned – texts, authors, critics, audience, institutions.

Buber can be said to fit into the philosophical traditions of Jewish mysticism and Phenomenology, the latter in that there are parallels with his work and that of Husserl and Heidegger.[6] As well as my above disclaimer that use of Buber is not intended to underwrite a theoretical project, it is also acknowledged that Buber himself does not write 'theory' in the general sense that the idea is understood. The turn to a relatively unappropriated writer with respect to literary studies and postmodern theory is an attempt to engage the notion of 'the Other' at a place that avoids a predictable insertion into the ongoing discourse. Further to this, rather than paraphrase Buber's philosophical/mystical treatise I will give the series of declarations that open the tract in full, since they contain virtually all of the potential material for what comes after in *I and Thou*.

> To man the world is twofold, in accordance with his twofold attitude.
> The attitude of man is twofold, in accordance with the twofold nature of the primary words which he speaks.
> The primary words are not isolated words, but combined words.
> The one primary word is the combination *I-Thou*.
> The other primary word is the combination *I-It*; wherein, without a change in the primary word, one of the words *He* and *She* can replace *It*.
> Hence the *I* of man is also twofold.
> For the *I* of the primary word *I-Thou* is a different *I* from that of the primary word *I-It*.
>
> Primary words do not signify things, but they intimate relations.
> Primary words do not describe something that might exist independently of them, but being spoken they bring about existence.
> Primary words are spoken from the being.
> If *Thou* is said, the *I* of the combination *I-Thou* is said along with it.
> If *It* is said, the *I* of the combination *I-It* is said along with it.

Alterity: Martin Buber's 'I-Thou' in Literature and the Arts 123

> The primary word *I-Thou* can only be spoken with the whole being.
>
> The primary word *I-It* can never be spoken with the whole being.
>
> There is no *I* taken in itself, but only the *I* of the primary word *I-Thou* and the *I* of the primary word *I-It*.
>
> When a man says *I* he refers to one or other of these. The *I* to which he refers is present when he says *I*. Further, when he says *Thou* or *It*, the *I* of one of the two primary words is present.
>
> The existence of *I* and the speaking of *I* are one and the same thing.
>
> When a primary word is spoken the speaker enters the word and takes his stand in it.[7]

We can begin formulating a philosophy with this question: is the relationship in Literature, between Literature and audience/author, an I-Thou or an I-It? I believe this is answered by recasting the question as follows: is our problem with Literature an ontological one, 'What is Literature?', or an ethical one 'What ought Literature to be?' (similarly Art). I would suggest that the answer lies somewhere along the following lines. Literature is ethical and philosophical in that when we ask 'What is Literature?' we are in effect asking 'What ought Literature to be?',[8] especially since theory cannot answer the question. In other words, the ontological of Literature *is* the ethical and philosophical. Hence, when Buber talks of the possible vacillation between the primary words I-Thou and I-It we can relate this to Literature as follows. We can say that the I-It, when applied to Literature, is actually the relationship between Literature and the theory of Literature, it is that relationship which pertains between Literature and audience/author when Literature is perceived to be in the realm of *things*. If this could be said to be the case for the whole complex entitled Literature, that is, if Literature were always an It and our relationship with it always deemed to be in the nature of I-It, Literature would present no problems for theory. But because this I-It is always changing into the I-Thou (or, more accurately, reverting to the I-Thou, since it is the I-It which is the real imposition) whenever Literature is talked about, whereby this alterity means that there can be no mastery, only in this infinite openness of the I-Thou (only as I-It can mastery of an Other [object] be achieved), can there be said to be Literature (Art).

Now it may be objected, amongst other things, that I have not spelt out exactly what or who is involved in the I-It and the I-Thou as regards Literature. It may also be objected that I have not stated whether I am proceeding by analogy or whether the relationships are meant to be taken literally, that is, are we speaking of an 'it is as if we were involved in an I-Thou situation' rather than 'we are so engaged'? Let us assume that Art/Literature is at some crossover point between analogy and literalness. By this I do not intend that we cannot decide, but that Art has its status precisely because it exists on this boundary between taking the primary words as analogous and taking them to be the fact of the matter in Art.

Another way to view this latter relation, which also relates to the first objection, is that in a particular – let us call it a matrix – involving Literature and an individual (a single reader/viewer/participant) we have the possibility of either I-It or I-Thou. Now the I-It is the theoretical relationship. There is no acknowledgement of reciprocity in the sense of that openness to alterity the I-Thou relationship involves. The I-Thou is Literature as replete, unlike the I-It. It explains the preference that lies in literary studies for what is more complex, 'deeper', since these notions desire, superficially at least, a state of affairs where immediate mastery (the I-It) is deferred in favour of a Literature that is beyond easy comprehension. That such a construction of the activity of Literature has political possibilities in terms of elitism is part of this, but not a necessary consequence. We should also distinguish between the openness of the I-Thou and talk of simply rehabilitating 'immediacy' over contemplation, that is, an attempt to valorise what is conceived to be immediately felt and/or understood (not necessarily the case for always) over 'intellectuality'. Such attempts at rehabilitation are usually given the most complex defences, for example when Antony Easthope appraises a 'Tarzan' novel in contrast to one by Conrad and argues that (to reduce the argument) the former should not be denigrated for appealing to an audience at a more sensory and less reflective level.[9] In terms of the I-Thou, what is immediately understood or felt, 'exhausted' (and I realise that this line of thinking is very unfashionable and has the pejorative connotations of a certain [Leavisite] morality – but given the drive to force ethics back into literary studies we should beware such knee-jerk dismissal) proceeds *against* the openness of the I-Thou relationship. This is not to say that Easthope is wrong in that more consideration might be given to Edgar Rice Burroughs – it might be that an I-It relationship has previously prevailed with respect to his work.

Inductively I take this preference for a Literature (Art) that constantly opens out as symptomatic of the I-Thou relationship that underwrites Literature (Art) (Easthope's claim might also be seen to be a claim for an openness). Similarly, Literature that is regarded as too obscure or 'difficult' remains at risk of being altogether too 'Other'. This in itself may be viewed as a radical otherness that makes the participant aware that the boundary is indeed a boundary and that the openness of the I-Thou is inhibited. The relationship in this particular matrix is thus an I-It, there being no reciprocity, only a reification into the Obscure. In this sense, then, good Literature is/has been that which appears to be constantly within the I-Thou (it 'speaks to us' rather than 'speaks at us'). Only by maintaining the I-Thou is Literature thus authentic; only when theory throws up its hands and acknowledges that the attempt to totalise is an attempt to make Literature inauthentic and to ignore that the I-Thou rather than the I-It is the primary relationship will it really be able to approach Literature. Nor is this argument applicable just to the *study* of Literature, it refers to the whole matrix of readers, writers, listeners, critics, theorists, biographers and texts that constitutes Literature.

This way of speaking about Literature – the Other, authenticity, I-Thou – strikes me as out of kilter with what might legitimately be said *at present*. As philosophy or ethics or mysticism it undoubtedly fits into the roll call of philosophers involved in Existentialist thought, and what has been appropriated from them by literary theory. Nietzsche, Heidegger, Husserl all stand behind both Existentialism *and* those in literary theory such as de Man and Derrida (and note too Levinas's indebtedness to those philosophers within the roll-call). Another pigeon-hole might be that of the 'dialogicians' identified by Michael Theunissen in *The Other*.[10] He notes that 'the philosophy of dialogue' ('dialogicalism') as practised by Buber and many 'lesser philosophers' 'derives ego or self in some manner from an original encounter with a "Thou"'.[11] An alternative framework to that I have taken from Buber for 'the Other' is provided by Husserl, Heidegger and Sartre and their 'transcendental phenomenology' which 'Starting from the premise of the ego, seeks access to intersubjectivity by construing the Other basically as an "Other I" or alter ego.'[12] My preference for Buber is that the alternative provided by Heidegger, Husserl and Sartre, where they begin with the self in isolation and work towards the social sphere from this *a priori*, automatically leans towards the individualistic. Buber, on the other hand, begins with the social relationship, this is what pre-exists and cannot be gainsaid. Although superficially the two variations promote intersubjectivity, the strand of Heidegger et al. always possesses the possibility of breaking down into individual atoms, an alienation that can in effect deny the social. Whilst Buber's I-It must share some features with this, it still remains in essence a relationship in the social sphere.

However, to return to the I-Thou and Literature, is it really possible to take terms from 'existentialism' and apply them in this way? Can we really speak of 'authenticity' within the matrix of Literature, or as a limit on the matrix of understanding Literature, and of the 'inauthenticity' of much literary theory? Are not these terms simply two more allotropes, a reintroduction of the problem of what constitutes Literature, or comprehends Literature, as outlined at the very start of the book? After all, how can we possibly utilise a notion of Literature which asserts that Literature (Art) is to be located wherever the I-Thou relationship is extant? How would it be possible then to distinguish between the I-Thou of my confrontation with the Face of the Other (to conflate Buber and Levinas) and with a piece of art which I did not somehow have to define as an art object, where I did not have to separate it out as an entity to which I added myself or an audience or an author or an institution for deciding such matters? Does this not take us back to the desire for a universal anthropological given that could determine Art? Isn't the I-Thou precisely a universal anthropological given?

I am certainly not arguing that the I-Thou is universal, although Buber appears to, as does the whole philosophical discourse centred upon notions of 'the Other' or 'Being-in-the-world-with-others'. This may or may not be the case. I am quite prepared to accept that Art is culture-specific, even if it does appear to go across the majority of cultures encountered. My assertion is that Art is at once the manifestation of the I-Thou in that it exists *for* the I-Thou, and is predicated *upon* the I-Thou in that its assumption is that the I-Thou is a primary word in Buber's sense. In this way Art can be distinguished from a tree, for example, which cannot be said to be *predicated* upon the I-Thou, unless it is classified as God's Art, even though, according to Buber, the tree might be involved in an I-Thou relationship. The latter would be an example of where we are tempted to say that the tree is a work of Art.

This leads us into the realm of intentionality. To say that the tree is not Art (I will return to distinguishing Literature within Art) depends (God notwithstanding) upon the notion that we can distinguish what has been predicated upon the I-Thou and what has not. Whilst the tree is a natural form and (again God notwithstanding) cannot be said to have been 'intended', that is, predicated upon the I-Thou, what of those arguments closer to home, such as the 'bricks in the Tate'? Were they Art? I regard this as a 'limit' argument for our purposes in that it stands at the edge of what we want to regard as Art. At least, it appears to do so. The question as to whether it is Art is easily answered as 'yes' since we are in an I-Thou relationship as described above, that it is a manifestation of, and predication upon, the I-Thou. The question really being asked is whether it is good art or bad art. But this may appear that I am avoiding the problem that proved impossibly nutty in the first part – again: 'What is Literature?'

The question 'What is Literature (Art)?' throws us back onto the above notion of intention, which also needs to be reconceived. It should not be thought of (and when I say 'should not' I mean that given the premise that is predicated upon the primary word I-Thou we look for the limits of this formulation) as authorial intention as discussed in the first part. In asking 'What is Literature (Art)?' we are asking has there been a predication upon the I-Thou? We can now think this through in terms of de Man's notion of intentionality. We can differentiate between Art and the natural world (the equivalent to Buber's tree is de Man's stone in this formulation) as above; this is no problem. As to de Man's notion of differentiating between the intentionality that informs Art – it is autonomous, an end in itself, target-practice – and the intentionality that informs the hunter's aim at an animal, which is circumscribed by the intention to eat or to sell, this also does not provide a problem (ignoring the contradictions inherent in any case as worked through in the first part) since the I-Thou predication is not one of autonomy as so conceived. It might be said that each I-Thou relationship concerning Art and Audience (although this is phrased badly since the notion of Art always brings with it the notion of Audience) is a closed circle and thus autonomous. This would be to ignore the I-Thou nature, or to belittle it, since Buber's I-Thou is a primary relationship that has an infinity in openness and obviously so conceived cannot be gainsaid – unless it be argued that, in fact, the relationship is always I-It and that it is wishful thinking to believe that Art is predicated upon, or is the manifestation of the I-Thou. Given the accumulation of what has been so far said, the latter possibility does not seem plausible.

It was stated in Part I that Literature (Art) has to be distinguished (it is a logical necessity) by positing some kind of literary (artistic) intention. This idea still holds perforce in the domain of *theoretical* reasoning. The I-Thou manifestation and predication does not have the same status of necessity, although it does have an obvious structural affinity with this idea of intention. Such a homology between the two is possibly the easiest way to grasp the nature of the I-Thou manifestation and predication.

What of that intentionality, as described by Hirsch, which claims that authorial intention is the only form of validation in interpretation? This is not much of an issue given the I-Thou, since, just as theory reduces the I-Thou to an I-It, that is, stands in an inauthentic relationship with the Other of Art in order not to face the Otherness of Art – alterity itself – and theory's own vulnerability to what constantly exceeds it (I-Thou; Art) – to regard Art solely as determinable hermeneutics is likewise to condense the I-Thou into an I-It. But to explain this it would be necessary to turn to those areas which have been rejected by most recent theoretical work, and consequently made others feel nervous: the idea of Art being close to life, of it being affective (emotive), of the role (and importance of the role) of the imagination from all aspects.

Let us just look for now at one of those areas so recently exiled, the 'producers' or 'creators' of art, intentional authors, either considered singularly or collectively.

They too are in an I-Thou relationship. Like an audience, which for many reasons they cannot be separated from, they too must suffer or embrace – we have no guidelines as to which might be the most desirable response to the manifestation and predication upon the I-Thou primary word – the alterity of Art, knowing, consciously, subconsciously, subliminally, that the Art they produce, create, author, exists within the I-Thou matrix of Art, is a manifestation of the I-Thou and is predicated upon it. Likewise the audience in the Art matrix is in a double relationship with Art in that it is both in the relationship of being in an I-Thou (metaphorically, literally) with Art as Other, whilst knowing (consciously, subconsciously, subliminally) that this Art is itself predicated upon the I-Thou and is the manifestation of the I-Thou that, according to Buber, informs the human condition. The difference, if not already clear, between the secular I-Thou that constitutes in its various aspects Art, and the I-Thou of Buber, is that whereas the former is part of the *description* of the human condition, the latter simply *is*. The human condition is thus not a manifestation of the I-Thou, it *is* the I-Thou, and as such must precede our discussion of Art/Literature.

So here it is clear that, to use the older categories of immanence (for example, de Manian) theory/criticism and sociohistorical (external 'evidence', for example, Hirschean), neither is full enough to cope with the I-Thou of Art – or rather, does not acknowledge the impossibility of such fullness (immanence, authorial intention). Nor is this to misread Hirsch, who does not deny that the evaluative process exists, rather only asserts that the proper approach to meaning can be what the author intended. To separate in such a way however denies the I-Thou relationship, which is *primary*. In other words, Hirsch, like de Man, focuses upon a *part* which in its self-closure automatically disallows certain other features – after all, de Man does not disallow the openness of theory to more theory when he claims that 'the resistance to theory is theory itself', or deconstruction the openness of itself to more deconstructive operation. It is not therefore surprising that the self-closure of such theoretical work ('open' only in the sense that they are open to their own reasoning), given the I-Thou we have been talking of, renders literary theories as mutually incompatible, and hence, also, the incompatibility of theory with non-rational philosophy. They are not open in the sense of the openness of the I-Thou, but open only in the sense of infinite regress (irony, for example). Hirsch disallows evaluation as having any claim to the operation of interpretation of Art. But this is a pointless exercise. It would be like arguing for the importance of the meaning of the Thou in the I-Thou *at the expense of* the whole relationship. To regard it in these terms is to act in bad faith since the I-Thou is not a sum of two parts but a relation, both in Buber's work and as we are discussing it here.

How might the Knapp-Michaels (neopragmatist) argument fit in to all this? Again, as with Hirsch, this is something of an irrelevance in that the I-Thou of Art is an acknowledgement, through its whole predication upon the I-Thou, of an Other. Given the mysticism of the I-Thou, perhaps it could be argued that God was/is author. But this is not an obstacle. Any thing can function as the implied author, as Knapp and Michaels point out: the subconscious of psychoanalysis and some feminist theory; society in Marxism, New Historicism, feminism. It is only because of the underlying alterity that the audience (individual, collective) is faced with that such a range of authors can be implied in the first place. Just as with the whole range of theories that cannot theoretically coexist if their separate premises are true, or are said to be true, it is only by virtue of the I-Thou which is in excess of the I-It (although, strictly speaking the I-Thou is simply of another order and not the subsumer of the I-It) and underwriting the notion of author that we have a variety of approaches attempting to pin down a particular author. They are symptoms of a common cause, and this might be taken as further evidence of the way in which the second part is justified in speaking in such a fashion.

Thus far Part II appears to favour those approaches, theories and criticisms dependent upon information outside the text, as if the I-Thou (and even I-It) were really the sociohistorical side of the coin by another name. The objection remains that the text (art object) is autonomous, that it transcends individual perception, that qualities such as literariness are immanent in the text. The problem here is that if we view the argument as one of either I-

Thou *or* autonomy we have set up a false opposition. There are a number of 'refutations' (it might appear scientific but is not intended to be so). Firstly, I am inclined to say[13] that given the premise that Art is at once a manifestation of and predication upon the I-Thou, the argument for autonomy is actually conducted at several removes down the line from this. The issue hardly makes any sense, since it would depend entirely upon the world of things, the world of the It, not even an I-It relationship. 'Very well', the objection might continue, 'but I still maintain that there is a quality that makes Literature "Literature", and that the quality is "literariness" of some form or other, whether objectively verifiable or subjectively perceived. And what is this "literariness" if not some autonomous feature that eludes your I-Thou?' But – and it does not matter whether we take 'literariness' in its technical sense or some looser general sense – 'literariness' is a quality or function which is taken, in the technical sense, to give the 'stoniness of the stone' (defamiliarise) or distinguish it, in the general sense, from what is not literary or Literature. In the latter case it is simply another version of the good/bad in Literature, in that some want to argue that Literature is separated out because of some great literary quality ('literariness').

The former objection, that the qualities of Art exist in the autonomous realm is to say that either the Thou is completely Other (hence 'makes strange' – although surely this 'makes strange' has to be *for* someone, or, along similar lines, this too is an acknowledgement of the I-Thou in that Art is on its guard against transforming itself and being transformed into the I-It, since, as Buber states, any I-Thou might become an I-It); or that it is in the realm of things – the least probable line of this argument – or of a thing, that is, Art as a whole field in its own objective right. This would not prevent an I Thou relationship, but would not be the I Thou of Art (manifestation and predication), rather, it would be of the order of the I-Thou that Buber states can be entered into with the tree. We can say that arguments for autonomy and immanence fail on any one of the above objections, yet there is still nothing to stop a counter-assertion that Art is *not* this double of 'manifestation' and 'predication' upon the I-Thou, only that the I-Thou provides a far better explanation for the contradictions that theories of Literature have continually worked through (in the same way that Part I of this book attempted to do), better than one which wants to categorise Art purely as an It, with the structure and mechanics of a machine.

Put in this way suggests that we have an ethical choice, that maybe we can regard Art as 'out there' with its laws and limits, processes and products, a separate entity, a man-made tree, in fact, or that we can choose to have this philosophical relationship with Art (more properly, an ethical relationship in that we must ask ourselves 'which do we prefer?', but I will come to this later). This would in effect take us back to the start of the book, its abyss-mal framework of allotropes where, due to the lack of any grounding structure for this framework, we can choose either pole as the preferred one, or some 'dancing between' as an ongoing struggle, challenge or openness. Having said there are no guidelines, once the premise that there is a fundamental relationship of I-Thou that constitutes Art and upon which it is predicated is accepted, there is no *real* choice.

If Art is this doubleness of manifestation and predication upon the I-Thou, the I-It is to be regarded either as bad faith, inauthentic, or the failure at some particular point of the I-Thou, a reification of the I-Thou (it could be argued that there is the possibility of choosing 'bad faith' of course, which is why we are making an ethical choice). It is no good attempting, as was illustrated by the theoretical shortcomings of the first part, to argue against theory with another theory, or with the language of theory. No doubt there is some kind of subsuming going on in that the I-It might appear to threaten the I-Thou. But the I-Thou is primary, is the *raison d'être* of Art. Nor is there any purchase to be gained from attempting to deconstruct the primary of the I-Thou, as if the I-Thou were threatened at the margins by the I-It. The I-It is not the *opposite* of the I-Thou in Art, nor in Buber's scheme, in the sense of a binary opposition. The relation between the primary terms is at best asymmetrical, and most fundamentally of different orders (a problem with deconstruction is that it is always assumed terms in opposition are somehow logically commensurate). The I-Thou *is* a positive term, although this is not to state a full presence. It is a positive term in the sense that it escapes the net of oppositional logic, which is exactly why it *cannot* be theorised. To theorise would be to claim a complete knowledge of the Other, to assert an I-It. Hence we are in what I can only describe as a non-rational environment.

As I have repeatedly stressed there are no necessary consequences for regarding Literature in this way. At this juncture I will go as far to provide a working definition of Literature in the light of the above. It would be to say that Literature is written material existing as predication and manifestation of the I-Thou (this might however also serve to bring us nearer to understanding what artistic intention might consist of). Such vagueness is unlikely ever to provide the firm basis for discussing, studying and evaluating Literature. A defence for the study of Literature is sometimes couched in terms that it provides a good starting point for asking many questions across a wide range of topics – history, politics, psychology, language, aesthetics – exactly the kind of open-endedness the Formalists were kicking against in their search to found a science of Literature. Such a defence sounds as if it is a manifesto of the I-Thou, but, valid as it may be within the realms of pedagogy, it is really an argument that the study of Literature is a convenient location for interdisciplinarity. No wonder then that there is a trend for 'literary into cultural studies', which, I would suggest, probably *is* a better use of resources if Literature is so conceived, although I would be inclined to say that the notion of Literary Studies being transformed into Cultural Studies is really Literary Studies being turned into the sociology of Literature, another case of the I-Thou being turned into the I-It with even less space for acknowledgement of the I-Thou nature.

Also, is it not the case, as stated in the introduction, that a certain amount of imagination and creativity is involved in theory and criticism? Do not these amount to the I-Thou relation, especially in the light of certain critical practices? For instance, should not an essay such as Cixous's 'Sorties' be viewed in exactly such a way?[14] Yet it is difficult to see how these could be anything other than a type of critical essay. Its particular use of language, which would be regarded as atypical for criticism in its 'creative' aspects, is simply part of the larger critical argument it is making about language, gender and subjectivity. Likewise Derrida et al. Although they are predicated upon the I-Thou in their attempts to open out language and language use, and to make readers aware of the instability of language and meaning, they cannot be taken to be manifestations of the I-Thou since they still depend upon the critical knowledge and underpinning of what their critical and theoretical project is. Rather than shifting the balance so that criticism and theory are taken to be as creative as the primary literature they comment upon, the attempt to introduce the I-Thou manifestation and predication into criticism and theory betrays the desire to collapse the description of the thing into the thing itself, that is, to collapse criticism and theory into Literature, to turn the map into the territory, as they say. Having failed to turn the I-Thou of Literature into an I-It of mastery, rather than accept the disjunction, it claims that there is no difference, and that theory and criticism themselves can re-enact the generation of Literature. But is not the *study* of Literature *part of* what we call Literature in any case? Yes, since it is only natural that the I-Thou of Literature/Art generates debate and dialogue, but it should be remembered that it is the I-Thou that is intrinsic.

Now, if any one theory is really no more than an approach, a particular machine to put texts through and provide readings, is a philosophy of Literature any different? After all, philosophy as a discipline is hardly in any better condition than literary theory when it comes to deciding between alternative models. No single philosophy will be able to successfully claim *a priori* grounds in the current postmodern climate, and antifoundational philosophies leave us in no better a position from which to argue the case for Literature, since what possible grounds could I have for arguing the antifoundational nature of all discourse? It is very tempting to argue that my case for the I-Thou has been proved apodictically, that is, true by virtue of demonstration, as I have tried to do in the preceding remarks. I would hazard that it is indeed only supportable in such an empirical manner (empirical in the sense of experiential – but then this is the whole point – experience and the reflection of and upon experience). In the climate of an epistemological scepticism that has successfully challenged all systems of thought that believe themselves to be grounded, there is room only for negotiations, compromises and consensus. There is no room for absolutes. Is it therefore possible to demonstrate the I-Thou in a more particular way? This question can be partially answered by the following exploration of what is called 'impossibility fiction'.

8
Impossibility Fiction? IF only ...

The University of Central England on 3 July 1993 held a one-day conference based upon a category termed 'impossibility fiction'. Before the call for papers for this conference materialised I had not come across the phrase. Nevertheless, I found myself looking at the various categories of writing included on the blurb and attempted to find a common denominator which would account for them all (*see* Appendix). This was in preference to immediately hunting down its meaning in academic journals and scholarly articles. It was partly an exercise in attempting to retain the I-Thou instead of seeking out the I-It of mastery. I thought this might be done by refusing to let the category be reduced to the definition provided by the blurb: 'any fictional narratives that deal ostensibly with alternative worlds, or which foreground imagination, fantasy, desire, unreality or the unexplained'. The term intrigued me so much I wanted to know it in a way that, for the time being, evaded this discursive net, a net I presumed it had already been caught up in. Might it be possible to use and manipulate the phrase in a way that illustrates the I-Thou? In particular, might 'impossibility fiction' be construed so as to demonstrate the ineffable experience of Art/Literature – the gap between the reading experience and the knowledge of that experience? Rather than proceeding therefore with the discussion in a specifically logical and theoretical way, what follows is the attempt to delineate an 'impossibility fiction' that lives up to the aura of intrigue it invokes and suggests. This part takes the attitude of wanting to create an entity called 'impossibility fiction', one that is not simply interchangeable with the descriptive term provided by the conference

– 'alternative-world fiction' – and to see if it could possibly be illustrative of the I-Thou.

The initial attraction for the conference was, I suspect, that the term might draw together a number of disparate elements into an unexpected but determinable field, rather like the attraction of the phrase 'alternative-world fiction' itself. One candidate for the role of common denominator for the field is the notion of metaphor. This appears to provide the perfect rule of thumb for what might be 'impossibility fiction'. With metaphor's juxtaposition of items that cannot logically coexist in the real world, and with its compression of images into an imaginative space which defies or is destroyed by paraphrase, metaphor is itself the perfect analogue. Juxtaposition is not the right word to describe metaphor however. The definition is more apt for simile. Let us take the simile, 'Eric is like a tree'. The comparing word 'like' simultaneously acknowledges and separates out the similarities and differences of the terms 'Eric' and 'tree'. If we remove the word 'like' in order to change it to the metaphor 'Eric is a tree' we have something that is of an entirely different order.

It is at this point we enter the realm of what can only be called 'impossibility fiction'. We know 'Eric' is not a 'tree', it is simply not possible, yet we know or feel that it does contain that politically incorrect ideal 'truth', that somehow, no matter how impossible, Eric *is* a tree, that there, we have said it, and it cannot be more perfect. This is not to say that the metaphor does not also function in the manner of a poetic trope. What I am saying here is that it can be viewed as entering the same network of relations that writer, work and reader do when engaged in the activity of fiction (and I would extend the argument to all Art). More than this, metaphor by its very nature, when given this imaginational status, either culturally or analytically, must also outreach the notion of possibility from the author's and reader's points of view (as it was suggested Literature does), which is not the case if regarded as a poetic trope (since this fits into a pre-given scheme). This is not to exile the poetic connotations of metaphor. This aspect indeed makes the apparently irreducible nature of 'Eric is a tree' more easily comprehensible. If we find that a particular metaphor cannot be more perfect, it is because as soon as we begin to explain in what ways 'Eric' is and in what ways 'Eric' is not 'a tree' we lose the insight (the reading experience) – metaphor in this way is not understood analytically (again, a non-rational environment prevails). Instead, metaphor is irreducible, or, to use a completely untheoretical concept, it is magic (the chapter now continues to use the word 'magic' as often as possible in order to give it the air of a technical term). Allow metaphor the status of fiction and it then has to be thought of as 'impossible', something which is not necessary if we put it into the network of relations regarded as poetry (in the above sense). This kind of magic, which I am suggesting is a manifestation of the I-Thou, would be exactly what I want from IF and what the blurb, despite its call for the incorporation into academia of marginalised fiction, would appear to disallow.

Yet this reasoning only leads to a dead-end. If metaphor is, as we might say, one of the conditions of possibility for fiction (Art etc. – for fiction continue to read Art), then all fiction is impossible, since it inhabits this unreal space, and the phrase is hardly suggestive at all. It is nothing more than a vicious circle to take metaphor as a type of imaginative fiction in its broadest sense and proceed to argue that fiction, in a narrower sense, thus has the appearance of unreality and the magic of metaphor. The consequence of this line of thinking would be that 'impossibility fiction' could only serve to be the generic grouping of, primarily, science-fiction and fantasy-writing that the conference poster suggested. So to take metaphor as a starting point that could underpin the term can only entail someone saying that all fiction is impossible because it is always metaphorical in the first instance. It would also be a cul-de-sac because fiction itself has anyway so far eluded all attempts to categorise it, has escaped all attempts to give it an undisputed poetics, and remains as much in this sense 'impossible', much like a child is said to be impossible, that is, will not conform to any strictures (the relevance of this line of thinking to the I-Thou in that all Literature/Art outruns theories and poetics is self-evident). Just to put 'impossible' in front of 'fiction' therefore seems a redundant exercise all ways round. Again, IF might just as well be called 'science-fiction' or 'fantasy' or 'alternative-worlds fiction'. In order not to reach this conclusion and instead to reach out for that something more which the phrase suggests, maybe it is possible to use the theme of 'alternative worlds' or 'other worlds' as the common denominator, but in a way that escapes itself and retains the magic of metaphor. The allure of the impossibility of metaphors and their other worlds is surely close to what we could make IF into. After all, how can a man possibly be a tree? What is this other world Eric inhabits when he is one? What is the ontology of metaphor? And let us remember that just as there is no satisfactory all-embracing account of fiction, nor is there of metaphor. 'Eric is a tree' could generate endless theses and leave us none the wiser. 'Eric is a tree' is precisely an other world. But how to describe it? Then again, why should this matter?

Jeff Torrington's *Swing Hammer Swing!* (winner of the 1992 Whitbread Book of the Year) has in small part this issue of metaphor and other worlds. Its own formal resolution of whether to take this world or an alternative world as its starting point is quite illuminating. The novel is set in the Gorbals, in Glasgow, where its central character has taken a year out from trying to earn some money and is attempting to write a novel instead. The novel he is working on, he muses a few pages into the novel proper, might begin like this:

> There was once this deepsea diver who discovered a tenement building on the floor of the ocean. He went through one of its closes and found himself in a backcourt where the calm corpses of housewives with carpet beaters in their hands floated around.[1]

Now, if the novel *had* opened like that it could quite easily have taken us into the realm of an 'alternative world' where the Gorbals was some place to be discovered at the bottom of the sea. *Swing Hammer Swing!*'s own opening is indeed itself very similar. It begins:

> Something really weird was happening in the Gorbals – from the battered hulk of the Planet Cinema in Scobie Street, a deepsea diver was emerging. He hesitated, bamboozled maybe by the shimmering fathoms of light, the towering rockfaces of the snow-coraled tenements.[2]

The novel's actual opening and the possible opening can be differentiated as the difference between simile and metaphor, the use of 'something really weird was happening' functioning in the same way as the word 'like' in a simile. The actual novel we read is therefore saying it is 'as if' the Gorbals were underwater. The novel has decided to function as a simile. But why should Jeff Torrington come down on this side, on the side that uses the caution of simile, and not the side that would structure the book on the impossibility of metaphor? Why not go with the original idea of a subterranean world called the Gorbals? Why not, in other words, write the impossible fiction? At this level there is no difference, the two books would be interchangeable. The other world of a subterranean Gorbals would not be an other world at all. It would not really be magic but the same food with a different sauce. To look at it like this means that the category of science-fiction as an equivalence for the IF we are attempting to create fares rather poorly. The world and fiction of novels like Margaret Atwood's *The Handmaid's Tale* and George Orwell's *1984* are, like Torrington's hypothetical other Gorbals world, impossible only in the most prosaic way. Or, to use the terminology that abounds in talk of fantasy and sci-fi, the secondary world of these novels is not a million miles from our own primary world. If we want to discount them from IF in terms of metaphor, the tenor and the vehicle of their worlds are far too close. They are not really metaphors. But then maybe that is because they are not the hardcore sci-fi which is really and truly other-worldly. But then, this is not exactly what I want from the term IF. My desire is to make visible the I-Thou. Sci-fi in my reading always reflects back onto this world in some way, satirically, for example, and/or as utopia or dystopia, and is therefore easily delineated and comprehended (it lacks the I-Thou). Sci-fi is merely the creation of worlds replicated from this one, and I say 'merely' because I have to have something that is altogether different, that in its entirety approaches the magic and irreducibility of metaphor itself. Let me look at sci-fi here by way of a diversion to see how it falls short of what I desire from 'impossibility fiction'.

In a book called *The Rationality of Emotion* Ronald de Sousa uses a science-fiction scenario to illustrate a concept used in science called 'emergence'.[3] I would like to use this example in two ways. Firstly, the idea of 'emergence' itself in relation to metaphor, IF and science-fiction, and secondly (briefly) de Sousa's own use of a sci-fi vignette for explanation. So, firstly, 'emergence' is an idea that is used in scientific theoretical models. 'Emergence' is a property that something has if it cannot be deduced from its constituent properties but can only be known by empirical discovery.[4] 'In that sense' (de Sousa argues):

> emergence is to be expected at many levels of science. To see this, consider the following story. In the Beginning or shortly after, we are told, all was Helium Soup. Could E.U. (an Extra-Universal scientist) have predicted the future properties of gold on the basis of other properties of existing particles? I see no reason to think so – unless we are willing to endorse classical rationalism, in which case all truths could be deduced a priori.
> But what if E.U. is allowed complete freedom to experiment with new compounds? She might take bits of helium off in her TUTU (Trans-Universe Transport Unit) into a universe where the conditions would allow for the constitution of gold. Then she can simply observe what the properties of gold turn out to be. In this way she will discover a new property of helium particles, namely, the property of being capable of being constituted into gold.

A little further on de Sousa explains the story as follows:

> This account is intended to placate both the reductionist and the antireductionist. Reductionism is vindicated because the higher-level property [i.e. gold] is indeed explained by the lower-level one [i.e. helium]. On the other hand, the opposition is right in its claim that there is no conceptual sufficiency of the lower-level properties. Given the right empirical hypotheses, one can explain, but one cannot analyze or define, the higher in terms of the lower.[5]

Metaphor too might be considered as the transportation of elements from this world into an unreal or hypothetical world, just as in the story. And the quality of the metaphor 'Eric is a tree' might be considered as precisely that of the emergent, in that we can explain the higher term, that is, the metaphor itself, in terms of its lower terms, for example 'Eric' and 'tree', but not analyse or define it with these terms and their accompanying baggage to a necessary and sufficient degree. The metaphor cannot indeed be deduced from its constituent properties, it remains irreducible, magic – in which case we are witness to the I-Thou rather than the I-It. This also holds good with respect to the discussion on the Author as uniquely creating and with works of Art in the sense of uniqueness, although the differentiation de Sousa makes between the categories 'explanation', 'analysis' and 'definition' is not particularly clear. We can 'explain' a work in terms of its constituent elements (the disentanglement of history, psyche, society, etc.) but could not predict the properties of this mixture (we cannot predict the properties of gold from observing helium).

Given the preceding remarks there should be no confusion between 'impossibility fiction' as it is here described, and such literature as science-fiction and fantasy which have surface similarities because of their 'other world' characteristics: they are not of this nature, they do not have the quality of emergence but are fully explicable, definable and analysable in terms of their lower elements, that is, elements taken from the recognised world (although of course in terms of the broader argument, as Literature in general they are part of the I-Thou. Through the notion of IF I am simply attempting to outline in a more concrete way how we might understand the I-Thou in a particular instance). This ease of comprehension (I-It mastery) would have been the case if Torrington had set his Gorbals in the subterranean other world, it would not have had the quality of emergence. In terms of language, subject matter, epistemology and ontology, the other worlds of fantasy and science fiction may be self-sufficient – and they usually are internally coherent and are expected to be so[6] – but they are worlds which are either extensions of this one or are literalisations of metaphors. The latter point is made by Jacqueline Pearson when she talks of women's science fiction, but I take it to be paradigmatic of science fiction in general:

> Women's novels, or feminist theoretic, provide metaphors of gender difference which can be given detailed materiality in science fiction. The literal war between the sexes in a novel like

Joanna Russ's *The female man* is only a continuation in another form of the metaphorical war in women's novels from Aphra Behn's to Alison Lurie's *The war between the Tates*.[7]

In other words Joanna Russ's novel is simply a kind of translation in that it does nothing that these other, non-sci-fi novels do not also do. Similarly, the category of science-fiction known as 'cyberpunk' does nothing that a novel set amongst the underclass could not do: they are either electronically generated parallel worlds, or the material manifestations of such metaphors. They themselves do not have the magic 'other worldness' of metaphor. Their literalisations are the equivalent of paraphrase, ways of saying things 'in other words' or even 'in other worlds'. Such it is too with de Sousa's use of a science-fiction narrative to illustrate his point about emergence. His own scenario, like sci-fi in general, does not itself have those characteristics of emergence. It is designed purely to illustrate points concerned with the nuts and bolts of the primary world. At this point we are as far as ever away from creating the IF we desire. If fantasy and sci-fi cannot do it, what can?

Ann Swinfen, in her book *In Defence of Fantasy* distinguishes between those novels which utilise parallel worlds and those which create wholly secondary worlds, the prime example of the latter being Tolkien's *Lord of the Rings*, where an entire other world is created. Parallel-world fiction is that type of fiction where primary and secondary worlds coexist. Ann Swinfen has serious reservations about this type of fiction:

> [The fantasy of worlds in parallel] has neither the firm underpinning of realism found in the fantasy set entirely in the primary world [by which she means the type of fantasy-fiction involving 'talking-beasts'], nor the combination of imaginative freedom and logical discipline which shapes the creation of the pure secondary world fantasy. Two worlds seen in parallel tend to clash, to contrast too strongly, to work against each other – making one or the other less credible, or undermining the relationship between the two.[8]

Impossibility Fiction? IF only ...

But might it not be that within parallel-world fiction it is at the intersection of two worlds that we find the real impossibility of fiction and hence IF itself, the I-Thou meeting, the manifestation of the ontology of the 'in-between' of the I-Thou? Ann Swinfen takes the approach that it is incredibly difficult to write successful parallel-world fiction. She is probably right to argue that there needs to be this internal coherence for fantasy which is difficult to sustain in parallel-world fiction. But when it is successful, when it does balance two worlds that are mutually exclusive, could this be our 'impossibility fiction'? Let me take three quite different narratives that might fit the bill: Henry James's *The Turn of the Screw*, Kurt Vonnegut's *Slaughterhouse Five* and Angela Carter's *Nights at the Circus*.[9]

The two worlds in *Turn of the Screw* are the natural and the supernatural (we might also say the realist and the modernist, but that is another matter). With regards to the parallel worlds, the story gives an either/or situation, knowing that it cannot be resolved, that is, we either accept it *as* a ghost story or as a story of misperception/lunacy/solipsism. But for readers the story is deliberately ambiguous and allows us the more embracing explanation of *precisely* this ambiguity. The bigger picture, so to speak, *is* that the tale is about its own fictional status and the problem of fictional knowledge. It presents us with the paradox that within its own primary world the natural and the supernatural, or the real and fantasy, cannot coexist, it is an either/or event, yet within the secondary world of fiction, from the point of view of the reader, they do coexist, just as I described the operation of metaphor at the start of this chapter. Note that here I do not mean that it is the literalisation of any particular metaphor, although *Turn of the Screw* does also have this side to it in that it is continually turning the screw of effect, as it suggests in the fireside banter at the beginning of the tale. What I am suggesting is that in its very structural functioning of the coexistence of logically inconsistent elements it is a metaphor. For *Turn of the Screw* cannot both be a ghost story and the realist tale of someone who is mad, yet it is, the nature of fiction allows it, just as the nature of metaphor allows for 'Eric' to be a 'tree'. But I want to say that the *Turn of the Screw* is *not* 'impossibility fiction', the reason being that I believe we should incorporate another element into our definition, in keeping with the desire to find the I-Thou in observable operation – that of the ineffable, that which is always out of reach, beyond our grasp intellectually, or fictionally, or emotionally even. *Turn of the Screw* does not fit this description because it encompasses and circumscribes its own ambiguity, it stands in relation to itself as I-It, the reader can grasp the tale because it is about its own fictional status. It is the nature of fiction that makes it possible, and so from this angle we are not in the realm of the impossible. It is going to take something more.

When I first read *Slaughterhouse Five* some years ago I took it to belong to the same class of fiction as all of Vonnegut's early novels, that is, science fiction. You do not think twice about the ability of the protagonist to travel in time between decades, and in space between the planets Earth and Tralfamadore, it is all part of the contract that the generic expectations of science fiction set up between reader and text. Sci-fi and fantasy genres allow what is normally impossible to be possible. That is one reason why I do not find the term 'impossibility fiction' compelling when used in this way, in the manner the term was set up by the conference at the University of Central England. Not until I entered academia did somebody point out that an alternative reading of the novel would have it that the hero/anti-hero, Billy Pilgrim, was mad, and that this could account for Billy's time and space travel as the imaginings of someone with senile dementia. It appeared (appears?) to be an inclination amongst people who were content to marginalise fantasy and sci-fi that whenever a novel was difficult to read as a realist text in the canonic mainstream it could always be recuperated by claiming that the narrative was by or about someone insane. And of course, once the claim is made that the novel is about madness, this makes the novel somehow more worthy. Kurt Vonnegut's own statement some way into his career that his work should not be regarded as science fiction re-enacts this academic recuperation of the impossible. Yet neither reading of *Slaughterhouse Five,* as realist or science fiction, has prior claim because they both stem from this same urge, to nullify impossibility, to allow the impossible to be possible. A realist reading cannot allow the parallel-worlds of two planets to coexist, or the parallel-worlds of the past and present to coexist, so the realist reading says Billy Pilgrim must be mad. The generic science-fiction reading permits and even demands the existence of parallel worlds. In neither instance do we have 'impossibility fiction', even if we do have 'alternative world' fiction. And here I think is a crucial difference between the call for papers' presumption about IF and what, by wanting to demonstrate the I-Thou, this part can create as IF.

I suspect that the same difficulty applies to what is called 'magical realism' in that the generic marker always recuperates or allows the space for the possibility of the parallel worlds of magic and realism, or, to put it more prosaically, the world of fact and fiction. By the time we reach the 1980s this generic recuperation is well in hand, to the point where the novels are doing it themselves, as in Angela Carter's *Nights at the Circus* of 1984. It has a central character called Fevvers with wings just like an angel. It begins with Fevvers being interviewed by a journalist, Walser, who is out to establish whether the wings are real or not. In fact, the ambiguity is rather like that set up in *The Turn of the Screw* since we do not know what kind of novel we are in. If Fevvers is a con-artist with artificial wings then the novel is essentially realist. If, however, the wings are real then we are being entertained by magical realism. If readers had not gathered this for themselves the novel at a couple of points self-reflexively tells them the paradox upon which it is structured. One of those instances occurs when the train Walser has been travelling on has broken down and he has ended up in the company of some tribe:

> The Shaman listened the most attentively to what Walser said after a dream because it dissolved the slender margin the Shaman apprehended between real and unreal, although the Shaman himself would not have put it that way since he noticed only the margin, shallow as a step, between one level of reality and another. He made no categorical distinction between seeing and believing. It could be said that, for all the peoples of this region, there existed no difference between fact and fiction; instead, a sort of magic realism. Strange fate for a journalist, to find himself in a place where no facts, as such, existed![10]

If anything were a candidate for 'impossibility fiction' when defined as that literature which exploits the cusp of parallel worlds (possibly the 'in-between' of the I-Thou) and had a whiff of the ineffable it would surely be magical realism. Yet this quote from Carter's novel illustrates the difficulty of such demarcation in that, as with science-fiction and fantasy, the generic contextualisation can be seen to converge with the very notion of fiction itself. If magical realism is distinguished in the mode that *Nights at the Circus* distinguishes it, as being a region where there exists no difference between fact and fiction, this is surely in the nature of fiction in any case. In other words, it is in the nature of fiction to always allow for the impossible. Another novel by Angela Carter, *The Infernal Desire Machines of Dr Hoffman*, puts the case very succinctly when a character claims one of the Doctor's main principles is that 'everything it is possible to imagine can also exist'.[11] This points to the beauty of fiction in that it does allow for everything imaginable to exist, but also therefore to the redundancy of the term 'impossibility fiction'. So, where to from here? I see four possible ways ahead that would not automatically be this continual falling back and collapsing of IF into the very nature of fiction itself.

1. It might be claimed that the analysis of fiction and metaphor has been faulty because the analysis has been of the logical-analytical type when in fact this is entirely inappropriate. To subject the metaphor 'Eric is a tree' to the same methodological scrutiny of truth as an apparently similar statement such as 'Eric is a man' is to be categorically wrong. Metaphor calls for an analysis and poetics that stems from a contextual approach to metaphor rather than a submission to logic. However, I do not see that in the long run the provision of a different framework of analysis for metaphor would avoid once again IF converging with the nature of fiction itself.

2. IF might be that type of fiction we regard as violating its own internal coherence. This is not the same as that type of postmodern fiction that bares its devices or is metafictional. A more apt term would probably be 'unsuccessful fiction' or 'rubbish'. We would be saying that because something did not succeed as fiction on its own terms it therefore became impossible *as* fiction (it has not mastered itself *as fiction*, or as the fiction it sets itself up to be). Whilst

there might be a certain amount of interest in this idea, I do not see too much mileage from it in terms of IF.

3. We concentrate on that type of fiction that tends towards the sublime, that kind of fiction that has been called 'the literature of exhaustion', exemplified by the work of Borges, Nabakov and Calvino. Indeed, to talk of it like this suggests the I-Thou at work. This type of fiction is the literary equivalent of drawings by Escher with their impossible stairways and columns. The phrase comes from an essay by John Barth. John Stark summarises the essay thus:

> The identifying characteristic of the Literature of Exhaustion, he states, is that writers of it pretend that it is next to impossible to write original – perhaps any – literature. In other words, some writers use as a theme for new works of literature the agonizing hypothesis that literature is finished. 'Exhaustion', then, has two meanings in Barth's essay: one, that literature is, or is nearly, used up; the other, that, given its current condition, writers should invent and exhaust possibilities and thus create for literature an infinite scope. They can accomplish this latter purpose by writing about the present exhausted state of literature, thereby making their original hypothesis a paradox.[12]

However, this too probably takes us no great distance from other generic terms such as Patrick Parrinder's 'portmanteau novel' which Neil Cornwell says is a term

> intended to designate the complex, multi-levelled or multi-layered novel which has come to dominate the novel form in the second half of the twentieth century … . This may often conform to postmodernism, at least in McHale's terms of ontological preoccupation …[13]

4. The fourth possibility is more bizarre. Let us imagine that 'impossibility fiction' exists but is invisible, it is an 'invisible genre', and it is invisible in two ways. Firstly in that we are always looking for it but like the ineffable can never grasp it, or rather, it is that type of literature which we cannot recuperate by genre. This might be either as an individual, in which case we might come

across a novel which confounds all our expectations and categories and contexts, or within the study of Literature. In its temporary sublimity it would have the nature of epiphany. Like metaphor such fiction appears to tell you a truth yet in a way that cannot be explicated (and remember, for fiction we can read the Arts in general). Of course it would only remain 'impossibility fiction' until that time the fiction had been circumscribed either by the individual or institution and no longer defeated our ability to comprehend it, or at least classify it. An example would be the invention of the descriptor 'free indirect discourse' which came along to tame the pre-eminent modernist narrative technique derived from Flaubert, or other terms such as I have already used like 'the literature of exhaustion', 'portmanteau novel', or understanding the difference between modernist and postmodernist fiction as that between the dominant of epistemology and the dominant of ontology.

The second way we might term it an 'invisible genre' is in many ways related to the first but is even further from view and would be described by Calvino's own definition of literature: 'Literature is a search for the book hidden in the distance that alters the value and meaning of the known books; it is the pull toward the new apocryphal text still to be rediscovered or invented.'[14] In trying to define the inner motivation for Literature it seems to me Calvino is describing exactly what cannot be Literature, it is the Literature that does not exist, it is the fiction we are always headed toward but can never reach. So, of course, not existing, being an invisible genre, there can be no examples (my apologies). Such writers as Conrad, James, Joyce, Woolf, Pynchon, Marquez, Borges have arguably been such writers in the past, in that they did alter the conditions of possibility for fiction, but having recuperated them of course they cannot now be 'impossible' as such. What may, in terms of genre, have existed in the realm of the I-Thou because they had no genre, can no longer do so. IF is then a generic idea that is always future-oriented and exerts a pull on current fiction writing. It is the fiction out of reach. Such a continual tension between 'the new' and attempts to define and describe what appears as 'the new' is suggestive of literary theory's relationship with Literature as a whole. The impossibility of literary theory 'catching up' with its object or discourse is evidence of the I-Thou.

It should be stated that at this local level of exemplification the preceding argument only holds good for a certain type of fiction – that kind of fiction that does not stand in relation to the body of fiction or itself in terms of the I-It but rather in terms of the I-Thou. It is at this point the general argument of the I-Thou of Art/Literature and a particular manifestation of it must part company – although undoubtedly the whole thrust of Formalism and the argument about 'literariness' would foreground this inner motivation as some kind of defamiliarisation. The general and the particular part company because of Calvino's (and Part II's) reification of Literature (it would be the same argument for Art) and apparent neglect of the reader. What is not addressed is the reading (Art) experience. However, 'impossibility fiction' does demonstrate the ineffable experience of Art/Literature – the gap between the reading experience and the knowledge of that experience. Having shown that IF can be used as a term to designate a certain kind of Literature with an inner motivation predicated upon the ineffable, I would now like to address the problem of the argument as it appears at this juncture, and which might now be taken to be one of the major fault-lines between theorists and anti-theorists within literary theory and Literature – the very disjunction between the experience of Art/Literature and the manner in which it is talked about or theorised.

9
Despair, Enchantment, Prayer: A Conclusion

> Now I want
> Spirits to enforce, art to enchant,
> And my ending is despair
> Unless I be relieved by prayer,
> Which pierces so that it assaults
> Mercy itself, and frees all faults.
> As you from crimes would pardoned be,
> Let your indulgence set me free.
>
> *The Tempest*[1]

> He knew everything about Literature except how to enjoy it.
> *Catch-22*[2]

The book thus far has struggled to mediate theoretically between textual (immanence) and sociohistorical (contextual) theories, approaches, methodologies of Literature. It was successful to a certain degree by altering the conception of what text and context might mean, say, in terms of 'the author'. It was dogged all the way through by the question 'What is Literature?' And despite the critique of postmodernism and the conclusion that ideas of the postmodern are flawed along the lines of 'history' (or 'materialism'), it nevertheless remains the case that the *theoretical* arguments, if not always the *practical* consequences (in the world outside of academic discourse), of its antifoundationalism are persuasive. This led to rethinking the direction of the book (and literary theory) and to the switch of Part II, which, after its recognition of the limits of theoretical endeavour in any form in the Arts (within its own delimitations), attempted to find an escape route

Despair, Enchantment, Prayer: A Conclusion

by way of demanding a philosophy of Literature (Arts). It decided that the evidence was for a philosophy which took as an article of faith a belief in some kind of 'I-Thou' formulation. It used Buber for freshness and relevance to the current debate: he is relatively unknown, yet has obvious affinities with all criticism/theory/philosophy involved with 'the other' – Derrida, Bakhtin, de Certeau, Levinas. I believe that the 'I-Thou' has much going for it and yet, inevitably, it is still not enough (necessary but not sufficient). Let us face the facts head on.

1. We do not know what Literature is, or, we cannot construct a definition of Literature that is satisfactory. Theoretically it would appear to require recognition on the part of those involved – teachers, critics, authors, publishers, readers – of literary intention (which might subsume other intentions such as 'author's message') but this is unhelpful.

So, at the most basic level, there cannot be a theory of Literature since it would always have to ask the question 'What is Literature?' to which there is no satisfactory answer.

2. At a more abstract level, the very notion of a 'theory' is absurd. Nor can we really circumvent this difficulty by replacing it with 'method' or 'approach' since the objection would remain that they were theoretically informed, for example, close-reading might be deemed a methodology or approach, but it would still be informed by certain theoretical ideas of organicism and 'holism', ideas of cognitive psychology, linguistics, etc.

3. 'In the current postmodern climate', despite valiant attempts to (re)introduce notions of 'responsibility' (ethics, the Other, a [the] 'subject'), such attempts are always duplicitous in that they contradict (logically) their own fundamental (a word not without irony) groundlessness. Everywhere, at every assertive juncture, for example claims for basic rights like freedom and justice, or some notion of history, we can ask (since they are in effect asking us to authorise such demands) 'and how do you ground *that* value, *that* ethic?'. Demands for such things as an ethically responsible criticism merely show that postmodern theory is caught up in the current climate of political correctness. Most importantly, these

demands are not consequences of their own theoretical machinations. The chapter on postmodernism and history within this very book makes a claim for history that cannot be theoretically or logically grounded. It too is caught up in the PC climate.

4. The hope for an answer and grounding that has also haunted the question of 'What is Literature?' has been in the elusive form of some 'anthropological universal given' – again, people talk of freedom and justice; others might talk about love, although this is a grounding rarely encountered in academic discourse, despite its prevalence as a topic in Literature and Art ('sex' on the other hand has proved quite alluring). Yet there might be more reason for considering such explicitly 'human' qualities as a useful starting-point since the notion of Literature can be taken (should be taken) in the first instance as a 'human' endeavour. However, all in all, there are no 'anthropological givens' on the horizon that I can see universal agreement on (for example, gender is a culture-specific construct despite the obvious biological differences between male and female which might be said to be universal). Furthermore, Literature itself is specific to certain cultures only. Saying this, however, does not negate the thinking that led us to require a universal grounding.

5. Tangential to 3, if rationality (the Enlightenment project) has failed, there is a certain redundancy to the initial argument in terms of 'adding' to knowledge in the sense of 'progress' or 'advance'. It might avoid this trap by arguing it provides a different perspective without making claims that amount to the teleological aims of the Enlightenment, but this would be a case of pedantry rather than substantive difference.

If we do ditch rationality, presumably we are left with a choice of irrationality or non-rationality. 'Non-rational' and 'irrational' are not to be automatically assumed derogatory terms. Barthesian 'pleasure' (*jouissance*) is irrational. So too, I would argue, is de Man's irony. The non-rational might include belief and mysticism. *The Direction of Literary Theory* thus acknowledges that it cannot ground any of its claims (but then, of course, no one can), and that it may even contradict certain notions laid out at the beginning, particularly the 'sliding-scale' notion of probability and plau-

Despair, Enchantment, Prayer: A Conclusion

sibility. It could be argued that the situatedness of all such discourse entails the accountability to context, to the strictures and boundaries of such strictures in force in particular societies, cultures and communities. This entails the type of argument that is pragmatist and cannot be gainsaid – purely because it is a simple assertion that 'what is, is'. It is the complement of the other pragmatist notion that what works in the world is by definition true. Pragmatism can thus be seen to be underpinned by a rather mystical outlook just as much as a practical one.

So what is left, what can be done, what can be said?

Let me try to reformulate a position.

Literature exists without well-defined boundaries. It appears as some complex or matrix of authors, texts, publishers, educational systems and readers. The desire to define what constitutes Literature exists primarily within education and is at its most acute in academia. In the practical world of Literature there is no such necessity – people read novels and poetry, they watch drama – whether it is to be deemed Literature (or Art), and what its defining properties are, rarely matter. Even such a high-profile case as 'the bricks in the Tate' did not lead to a full-scale review of people's perceptions, since, in the non-academic world, for something to be Art carries with it a value judgement: 'The bricks in the Tate' were perceived by the majority not to be Art because they were no good, and, conversely, despite being in a context which signified Art, they were no good because they failed to achieve the status of Art.

The obvious objection to this is that Art and Literature are not natural phenomena; people have been educated in various ways to recognise these works as Literature and Art, so the argument goes, it is just that the criteria have been internalised. The education process is therefore open to scrutiny since that is where Literature and Art are, in effect, being produced. But this argument has only a limited validity. Just because people are educated to be literate does not mean that this process produces the phenomenon of newspapers. The existence of newspapers might depend upon literacy, but that is as far as the argument does go. The very existence of drama and poetry does not depend upon the education system, even if its livelihood does. Hence, the problem of 'What is "Literature"?' *is* purely academic. This, no doubt, to some people, will seem rather obvious. Be that as it may, the consequences are not self-evident. The existence of theory, the existence of Literature departments, the tradition of English Studies, can only be said to impinge upon Literature (and Art) in the most mundane way. Why an author writes and why a reader reads is a mystery, and no amount of empirical observation or hypothesising has brought us any nearer to solving it. Yet the reasons for the very existence of Art forms must lie with these desires. Where could we begin to analyse such desires? Through the lens of sociology? But the psychologists would object. Through a science of aesthetics, or a philosophy of aesthetics? But the scholars of politics would object, and quite possibly the sociologists. Etc., etc. What justification is there, therefore, for the study of Literature, Art or culture that is not, at the final analysis, implicated in the process and ideology of culture? Looked at like this, any assessment can only be given value by the system it is part of. Therefore, what value can such studies have? And if this is the case, the value determines the definition. In one sense this returns us to Pinkney's forecast, that the future of literary theory depends upon its value for pedagogy. There is another scenario whereby literary theory continues in Cultural Studies, or Critical Studies, and is hence circumscribed by a different set of values, yet just as unlikely to be able to describe the functioning of Literature.

THE REAL RETURN OF VALUE AND PEDAGOGY

We do not necessarily study Literature because people enjoy it – yet that may be its prime ontological foundation. As stated above, if this is so, it does not appear that we will ever be in a position to understand it on its own terms. We study it because we presume it has some value. Immediately, therefore, there is a disjunction. We are approaching it from a viewpoint that has a set of criteria not intrinsic to its materiality. Much of our failure and difficulty has been this incommensurate, or unacknowledged, imposition of value onto enjoyment, not that the two are necessarily antithetical. What is the value of enjoyment? If it were possible to formulate an understanding of that question then Literary Studies would be saved in some form like its present. But enjoyment exists, or can exist, without value, at least value in the sense of having value for study, that is, it exists as an end in itself, the value is psychological or spiritual or biological in a way that cannot be captured. Literature (Art), as the complex or matrix in the non-academic world described above, cannot be defined, except as some description of current and past material practices, a definition that would have to be changed every few hours like a baby's nappy. No, the only way to define Literature, since it doesn't exist, if we are to be fully aware of the matrix, is in terms of its value for study. This will reintroduce the factors that form the matrix – authors, texts, language, audience, education, etc. – but only within the understanding of the value it has for study. Any other claims to know what Literature is without this circumscription is to speculate in terms that exceed the condition of possibility for studying Literature.

The book is still not out of the fire since the suggestion now is that it can define Literature, albeit in reduced circumstances.

Firstly, in order to proceed, we might regard Literature as a blik. What is a blik?

> The word is R. M. Hare's and signifies any deep conviction which is not susceptible to verification or falsification. Moreover, a *blik* does not constitute an explanation, as it is precisely that by which we decide what will or will not count as an explanation.[3]

It should be remembered, that even when we decide on our belief about Literature in the academic environment, we are still circumscribed by our attachment to value. My enjoyment and response to Literature is irrelevant for what I decide to say within the academic establishment. This is precisely what is in excess of literary studies. My personal value system is of no interest to what I say about Literature, *except* under the umbrella of the more general value system embodied within the discipline. What I am about to say should be understood as still circumscribed by this notion of Literature being both a blik and a value-dependent notion within education.

Literary studies has two main strengths. Whether defined in existential, psychological or societal terms, simply and simplistically,

Literature provides enjoyment for a large number of people and provides insight (or perspective if you prefer) into the human condition. If we are to talk of value, surely that is the starting point.

To return to literary theory, I find theory interesting as a discourse on its own terms, virtually divorced from the experience I get from reading and experiencing Literature. I also feel, and I do not know if this is a common experience, that my knowledge of theory has impinged little upon my so-called innocent reading. But I do see how knowledge of any of the theories I have previously mentioned *can* add to my understanding of Literature – I do see that I might view, New Critical fashion, a work of art as a well-wrought urn, and I do see that I might view a text through the eyes of New Historicism and see it as part of a much larger social and cultural text, and find that in turn interesting, but only by virtue of the fact that they will feed back into what I can only vaguely call the reading experience, as well as providing further understanding (or different perspectives) on the human condition. It should be understood that the actions and thoughts of such things as characters is of interest and open to debate, that the relationship between the author and his or her work is a site of interest, as is the relationship between art and life, because we live in a world where people with an actual historical existence create, for whatever reasons, works of art for audiences, themselves with an actual historical existence, to enjoy and experience and learn from. And it is often the case that people believe that these works of art speak to them in a real and significant way (the I-Thou), tell them something about themselves, about other lives, give them ideas, enable them to understand things, all the old-fashioned things Literature and Art were expected and presumed to do (again, the I-Thou). We let theory belittle these experiences at the risk of losing student's interest in Literature. Helen Taylor describes the divide between Higher Education and the schools teaching the students who go on to study in these establishments as precisely this disjunction between what is felt permissible.

> Rarely are English teachers given the credit due for the increasing numbers of English and cultural studies applications to colleges and universities, as well as the radical rethinking of examination and assessment modes. Accepting the English lesson as the

one clear curriculum space in which students' emotional, intellectual and political experiences, questions and doubts may be explored through those imaginative responses university lecturers are nervous about, schoolteachers have continually experimented with ways of contextualising both language and literature.[4]

If theory is put into this context, if it is naturally subordinated to the reading experience, to the I-Thou underwriting Art, and the excitement and interest generated by it, then I do not see any problems for the teaching of theory. For a student not to want to do theory in their Literature degree would then be no more heinous a crime than someone not wishing to study Shakespeare. The whole project of literary theory has deemed itself essential to Literature and the study of it. This should not be the case unless we are to alter reading of Literature into a purely technical exercise, as we have seen Tony Bennett demand, or see it in terms of sociology, as Cultural Studies demands.

Leicester University, for example, appears to have listened to the demands and wishes of its students. The academic year 1993–94 saw a shift in the way it taught theory. In the past one theory after another had been lectured upon, starting with Formalism, working its way through structuralism, feminism and New Historicism. It was left up to the individual tutor as to whether they looked at what are called primary texts in the light of these theories. Theory was thus treated as a discourse of its own. The revised course instead takes three primary texts – Plath's *Ariel*, Conrad's *Heart of Darkness* and *Hamlet* – and allows tutors to bring in theories as and when they choose. This is perhaps the way forward if people are determined to keep theory within the study of Literature in that its focus remains the Literature, rather than the occasional use of Literature to prove a theory. But a note of caution should be sounded even here. There is already a book on the market which prints the text of Conrad's *Heart of Darkness* and follows it with a variety of theoretical readings: New Historical, psychonalytical, etc.[5] This is an increasing trend but I think this too is a mistake in that it simply substitutes the claim of a single dogma, as we might have had in the past, for a few dogmas more. Once again the reading experience is ousted by a sequence of pseudo-theories. Surely it is the reading experience and our desire for knowledge into the human condition that should inform our study of Literature to a greater rather than lesser extent, and that should be the context within which theory operates. By human condition it is not meant the 'human subject' in humanist terms. It simply means that Literature is one practice amongst others that provides a place for discussing and analysing human existence, and is more often than not its dominant concern. This is one of its values for the study of Literature as it is circumscribed by the larger cultural concerns of academia and society.

To conclude I would like to identify three positions that the work of this book has made available (or believes are available), positions apparent in Prospero's summation of his magical project at the end of *The Tempest*: despair, enchantment, prayer.

Despair

The book agrees with antifoundationalist arguments of the neo-pragmatists. The consequence does not have to be nihilism or despair – it can simply be acknowledged that this is how things are, theoretically speaking, and that the world continues to be the world irrespective of the theories that attach themselves to it. This does not mean that theory has no use. It simply means that any particular 'theory' is a self-consistent approach or way of seeing something (texts, physical objects, power) and we should be aware of this and particularly wary of metatheories. This awareness would acknowledge that the demand for self-consistency may in itself be an obstacle to understanding complexes drawn into the discursive fields we wish to explicate, and would also acknowledge that our understanding is not necessarily commensurate with what we wish to study. It does mean, however, that Literary Theory is from the outset a conglomeration of heterogeneous, *incompatible* perspectives. Whilst these perspectives are 'rational' (or aim to be), I would go as far as saying that the umbrella term 'Literary Theory' and the project it embodies is 'irrational'. To devote ourselves purely to Literary Theory is, therefore, to invite despondency, since it can be nothing other than a failed project. Interest in Literature is not a consequence of theory. Nor should we believe that we can understand Literature through theory. This too is irrational. Instead I would want to promote a mixture of the final two positions, 'enchantment' and 'prayer'.

Prayer and Enchantment

This identifies the philosophical position – a belief in the I-Thou, with Art manifested and predicated upon it. We would proceed hopefully (on a wing and a prayer) on this basis: this is what relieves us from the imprecations of antifoundational logic (and it *is* logical, after all). The attitude of 'prayer' ('hopefulness') is essentially the position of the last two chapters. Coupled with this is an acknowledgement of the 'enchantment' we find in Literature (Art) – we are in its thrall, we cannot escape that. I suggest therefore we proceed under the sway of the I-Thou, under the sway of an ethical drive, acknowledging that we cannot ground our ethics at a theoretically satisfactory level. We will, in our desire to understand Literature, have to note the 'reading experience' as being similarly beyond any permanent (or even half-satisfactory) theoretical formulation – yet *base* our understanding upon this (hence non-rational), along with an acknowledgment that there is a certain creative (imaginative) uniqueness to works of Art, or at least the possibility of such. Hence the return of the Author, although this is not to say that meaning is confined to author intentions (which are plausibly recoverable and articulable) but because 'intention' is a variable quality also locatable elsewhere (and here may be the value of the self-consistency of theories). The notion of uniqueness should also signal the return of evaluation, of a willingness to say that on these grounds some artistic works and some ideas are more valuable than others. This is how we might begin to say what we want Literature to be and how we want to study it, teach it, read it, and live with it.

Appendix

CALL FOR PAPERS

Impossibility Fiction
An Academic Conference on the Literature of Fantasy and SF
School of English, UCE
3 July, 1993

In recent years, the academic exploration of fantastic and science fictional texts has become more popular and more acceptable in the mainstream of literary studies. The effect of this has been to draw literary critics, philosophers, cultural analysts and scientists into a common discourse. As an opportunity of furthering this debate, a conference has been organised to provide a space to reflect upon the significance and meaning of this major strand of our literary cultural life.

The phrase 'impossibility fiction' is intended to be a generic term covering any fictional narratives that deal ostensibly with alternative worlds, or which foreground imagination, fantasy, desire, unreality or the unexplained. It encompasses fantastic and science fictional texts from all periods of history and across all cultures and disciplines. And it includes the impossible as a conceptual framework in texts that claim to be non-fictional. It recognises that the definition has as much to do with readers' perceptions as with textual features.

'Impossibility fiction' is inherently multi-disciplinary and has escaped many of the traditional literary categories by being so long regarded as 'inferior' literature. It is expected, therefore, that conference participants will come from a variety of disciplines, and will represent various fields of inquiry, including science, literary studies, film and communication studies, social science, education, writing, reading and cultural criticism. Participants not affiliated to academic institutions, post-graduate students, and final year degree students will be equally welcome.

Appendix

Papers and seminar sessions are invited dealing with any aspect of relevance to the conference theme. Workshops and panel discussions will also be welcomed. It is envisaged that subjects covered might include the relation of impossibility fiction to the mainstream, experimentalism in form and concept, issues of science, rationality, imagination and fantasy, the nature of reality and fictionality, the reception of fantasy texts, studies of individual authors and works, religious or mythic narratives, medieval and renaissance fantasy, dream texts, drug-induced narratives, utopias, the gothic, horror, magical realism, cyberpunk, folk literature, fairy-tales, theoretics of fantasy literature, pulp or transitory fiction, children's literature, escapism, wish-fulfilment, psycho-analytical interpretations, fantasy in film, television and graphic form.

Presentations should be planned for a one hour session, to include an opportunity for discussion. An abstract, typed on one side of A4, should be provided in advance.

Notes and References

1. Introduction

1. Patrick Parrinder, 'Having Your Assumptions Questioned: A Guide to the "Theory Guides"' in Bradford, ed., *The State of Theory* (London: Routledge, 1993), p.135.
2. Friedrich Nietzsche, *Genealogy of Morals* in *'The Birth of Tragedy' and 'The Genealogy of Morals'*. Translated by Francis Golffing. (New York: Anchor Press, 1956), p.255.
3. See Antony Easthope's 'Paradigm Lost and Paradigm Regained' in Bradford, ed., *op. cit.*, p.92.
4. James Kirwan, *Literature, Rhetoric, Metaphysics: Literary Theory and Literary Aesthetics* (London: Routledge, 1990), p.1.
5. ibid.
6. ibid., p.2.
7. ibid., p.5.
8. ibid., p.6.
9. ibid.
10. Raymond Tallis, *Not Saussure: A Critique of Post-Saussurean Literary Theory* (Basingstoke: Macmillan, 1988).
11. Christopher Norris, *What's Wrong With Postmodernism: Critical Theory and the Ends of Philosophy* (New York: Harvester Wheatsheaf, 1990).
12. William Ray, *Literary Meaning: From Phenomenology to Deconstruction* (Oxford: Basil Blackwell, 1984), p.20. There is an analogy between this notion and 'chaos theory' which posits that there can never be enough information known or taken into account to fully describe a system.
13. David Lehman, *Signs of the Times: Deconstruction and the Fall of Paul de Man* (London: André Deutsch, 1991), pp.84–5.
14. Roland Barthes, 'The Theory of the Text' in Robert Young, ed., *Untying the Text: A Post-Structuralist Reader* (London: Routledge, 1987), p.35.
15. Ray, *op. cit.*, p.1.
16. ibid., p.2.
17. Ian Hunter, *Culture and Government: The Emergence of Literary Education* (Basingstoke: Macmillan Press, 1988), pp.viii–ix.
18. ibid., p.viii.
19. If readers are unhappy with this, I would refer them again to William Ray's critique already mentioned. Likewise, Steven Knapp and Walter Benn Michaels identify 'theory' as 'a special project in literary criticism: the attempt to govern interpretations of particular

texts by appealing to an account of interpretation in general'. However, they also argue that prosody, stylistics and narratology are 'empirical' and thus do not fall into this category, 'Against Theory' *Critical Inquiry* 8 (1982), p.723. I would say that these too, despite their aspirations to a transcendent poetics, come under interpretation. This might be observed in the discussion of de Man's notion of intention in Chapter 3. De Man begins by discussing aesthetic structuring but is drawn inexorably to subordinating this to hermeneutics.

20. Ray, *op. cit.*, p.141.
21. An analogous difficulty occurs in linguistics in that the search to understand 'language' can only be made with the use of language; in philosophy an analogous problem is the attempt to solve the notion of Becoming (process) through positing Being (structure); in psychology we can only solve the issue of consciousness through the workings of our own consciousness. It is even tempting to say that I am seeking to resolve the problem of Literature, which I have to posit, with Literature.
22. Jerome J. McGann, *Social Values and Poetic Acts: The Historical Judgment of Literary Work* (Massachusetts: Harvard University Press, 1988), pp.112–13.
23. Quoted in Robert C. Holub, *Reception Theory: A Critical Introduction* (London: Methuen, 1984), p.4.
24. Steven Connor, *Postmodernist Culture: An Introduction to Theories of the Contemporary* (Oxford: Blackwell Publishers, 1989), p.15.
25. Ian Small and Josephine Guy, 'English in Crisis (2)', *Essays in English* 40.3 (1990), p.196.

PART I

2. Making the Author Function

1. Italo Calvino, *If on a winter's night a traveller ...* (London: Picador, 1982), pp.126–7.
2. Roland Barthes, 'The Death of the Author' in *Image/Music/Text* (London: Fontana, 1977). Essays selected and translated by Stephen Heath. First published as 'La Mort de l'Auteur', *Manteia* V, 1968.
3. See E. D. Hirsch Jr, *Validity in Interpretation* (New Haven: Yale University Press, 1967).
4. Paul de Man, *Blindness and Insight: Essays in the Rhetoric of Contemporary Criticism*. 2nd edn, revised. Introduction by Wlad Godzich. (London: Methuen, 1983), p.35.
5. Herman, Luc, Kris Humbeeck and Geert Lernout, eds, *(Dis)continuities: Essays on Paul de Man* (Amsterdam: Rodopi, 1989), Introduction, p.11, quoting Jeffrey Mehlman.

6. It is also worth noting the more recent controversy surrounding the discovery of racist and sexist material in Philip Larkin's legacy. It serves further to illustrate that 'theory' has failed to remove our desire for information about authors, that, in fact, theory in this area has had no consequences, although obviously this is in no way meant to stand as a theoretical refutation. The lack of consequences for theory is a point the book returns to.
7. Barthes 'The Death of the Author', *op. cit.*, p.142.
8. *ibid.*, p.145.
9. *ibid.*
10. *ibid.*, p.146.
11. Patrick Colm Hogan, *The Politics of Interpretation: Ideology, Professionalism, and the Study of Literature* (New York: Oxford University Press, 1990).
12. Raymond Tallis, *op. cit.*
13. Patrick Colm Hogan, *op. cit.*
14. In Rabinow, *The Foucault Reader* (London: Penguin, 1986).
15. *ibid.*, p.108.
16. *ibid.*, p.113.
17. *ibid.*, p.109.
18. *ibid.*
19. *ibid.*, p.110.
20. *ibid.*, p.118.
21. *ibid.*, pp.118–19.
22. *ibid.*, p.120.
23. Jules Siegel, 'Who is Thomas Pynchon ... and Why Did He Take Off with My Wife?', *Playboy* 34 (March, 1977), pp.97, 122, 168–70, 172, 174.
24. Steven Weisenberger, *A 'Gravity's Rainbow' Companion: Sources and Contexts for Pynchon's Novel* (Athens: University of Georgia Press, 1988).
25. Lehman, *op. cit.*, p.158.
26. *ibid.*
27. Frank Lentricchia, quoted in Lehman, *ibid.*, p.149.

3. Intention in Literary Theory

1. 'Murder Case Man's "Threat" to Shoot Teddy Bears', *Guardian*, 11 March 1992, p.2.
2. In fact I find it both funny *and* tasteless.
3. Colomb, Gregory G. and Mark Turner, 'Computers, Literary Theory, and Theory of Meaning' in Ralph Cohen, ed., *The Future of Literary Theory* (London: Routledge, 1989), p.407.
4. Wimsatt, W. K. R., Jr, and M. Beardsley, *The Verbal Icon: Studies in the Meaning of Poetry* (Kentucky: University of Kentucky Press, 1954).
5. *ibid.*, p.3.

Notes and References

6. In 'The Affective Fallacy', *ibid.*, p.21.
7. *ibid.*, p.3.
8. *ibid.*, p.4.
9. *ibid.*
10. *ibid.*, p.10.
11. *ibid.*
12. *ibid.*
13. Hirsch, *op. cit.*
14. De Man, *op. cit.*
15. Hirsch, *op. cit.*, p.5.
16. *ibid.*, p.6.
17. *ibid.*, p.39.
18. *ibid.*, p.67.
19. *ibid.*, p.13.
20. I would actually cite the work of The Prague School as first treading this path.
21. De Man, *op. cit.*, p.21.
22. *ibid.*, p.22.
23. *ibid.*, p.24.
24. *ibid.*, p.25.
25. *ibid.*, p.26. If we followed the logic of de Man's argument then the threat to shoot teddy bears would be the act of someone interested only in aesthetics.
26. We might also query if there *can* be such a thing as aim-taking for its own sake – must it not always fulfil some desire, need or use on the part of the person taking aim?
27. *ibid.*, p.27.
28. *ibid.*, p.29.
29. *ibid.*
30. The work of Jan Mukarovsky and his notion of 'structure' might have provided a way out of this for the argument that de Man is proposing, especially when Mukarovsky states that: 'The work ... is not an unambiguous structure' in Peter Steiner, ed., *The Prague School: Selected Writings, 1929–1946* (Austin: University of Texas, 1982). There is usually an assumption that although the meaning of a work is variable, a description of its basic structure or pattern is not, yet surely what we take to be 'the skeleton' of a work (the 'plot' of a novel; the 'dramatic' development of a play) is itself, as Mukarovsky points out, a question of interpretation.
31. De Man, *op. cit.*, p.29.
32. *ibid.*
33. *ibid.*, p.30. 'Richness' is an interesting word to use. Is this the spectre of liberal-humanist criticism haunting the house of structuralism?
34. Steven Knapp and Walter Benn Michaels, *op. cit.*

35. W. J. T. Mitchell, ed., *Against Theory: Literary Studies and the New Pragmatism* (Chicago: The University of Chicago Press, 1985).
36. *ibid.*, p.5. Although from what we have seen, in de Man it is not clear whether the text works on the reader or vice versa.
37. *ibid.*
38. Knapp and Michaels, *op. cit.*, p.727.
39. *ibid.*, p.728.
40. *ibid.*
41. 'A Reply to Our Critics' *Critical Inquiry* 9 (1982–83), p.798.
42. *ibid.*, p.799.
43. Tony Bennett, *Outside Literature* (London: Routledge, 1990). One of Bennett's faults is to see the problem in terms of *English* Literature, which carries with it all the connotations that Bennett would like to rid it of. Surely this would not be the case if the subject were just called 'Literature'?
44. Antony Easthope, *Literary Studies into Cultural Studies* (London: Routledge, 1991).

4. Postmodernism and History

1. A version of this chapter appears in Earnshaw, ed., *Postmodern Surroundings* (Amsterdam: Rodopi, 1994).
2. Steven Connor, *op. cit.*, p.45.
3. Huyssen: 'The problem with postmodernism is that it relegates history to the dustbin of an obsolete épistème, arguing gleefully that history does not exist except as text, i.e., as historiography' *New German Critique* (Winter 1981) 22, p.35; Foster: 'To put it crudely, this Postmodern Style of History may in fact signal the disintegration of style and the collapse of history' *New German Critique* (Fall 1984) 33, p.72; Jameson talks of postmodernism as pastiche and the 'loss of depth' as indicative of a loss of a sense of history, *Universal Abandon*, ed. Andrew Ross, p.4.
4. Docherty's line of reasoning can also be found in his essay 'Theory and Difficulty' in Bradford, ed., *op. cit.*.
5. 'Thinginess'. Docherty uses the Greek word *haecceitas*, which Steven Connor defines as what is 'unassimilable and untranslatable "thisness"' in Bradford, *op. cit.*, p.40.
6. Jean-François Lyotard, *The Postmodern Condition: A Report on Knowledge*. Translated by Geoff Bennington and Brian Massumi. Foreword by Fredric Jameson. (Manchester: Manchester University Press, 1984), p.xxiv. The phrase has become axiomatic within discussions of postmodernism.
7. Brook Thomas identifies a second strand of New Historicism, that associated with Jerome McGann in *The New Historicism and Other Old-Fashioned Topics* (Princeton, N.J.: Princeton University Press, 1991).

Notes and References

8. H. Aram Veeser, ed., *The New Historicism* (London: Routledge, 1989).
9. Elizabeth Deeds Ermarth, *Sequel to History: Postmodernism and the Crisis of Representational Time* (Princeton N.J.: Princeton University Press, 1992).
10. Thomas Pynchon, *Gravity's Rainbow* (London: Picador, 1975).
11. ibid., p.164.
12. ibid., p.328.
13. ibid., p.612.
14. An equivalent problem might be David Irving's version of the Second World War and the consequences of having no ground upon which to judge his views as incorrect. He has argued that Hitler did not know about the holocaust. Perhaps even more pressing is the need to counter neo-Nazis who insist that the holocaust never happened. I deal with this later in the chapter.
15. Brian McHale, *Postmodernist Fiction* (London: Methuen, 1987), p.91.
16. ibid., p.96.
17. I am thinking in particular here of Linda Hutcheon's attempt to define postmodernism as 'metafictional historiography' in *A Poetics of Postmodernism*, a definition which, like McHale's, would like the ethics of history alongside an irreverence towards totalising establishment paradigms. Linda Hutcheon, *A Poetics of Postmodernism* (London: Routledge, 1988).
18. McHale, *op. cit.*, p.96.
19. Ann Rigney, 'Review of Lionel Gossman's *Literature and History*' *History and Theory* 31.2 (1992), p.216.
20. Michael Burns's review of current trends in history states that:

    more recently, critics interested in poststructuralism and deconstruction have maintained that historical 'narrativity' is not only ideologically bound but a way of writing that is itself 'imaginary' and fundamentally no different than fiction. No mode of discourse is purely objective, goes this argument, and least of all narrative history, that artificial reconstruction of events connected only in the fertile imagination of the architect.

    Michael Burns in Geoffrey Barraclough, *Main Trends in History*. Expanded Edition. (New York: Holmes and Meier, 1991), p.228.
21. Pynchon, *op. cit.*, p.56. This reads as a prefiguring of Docherty's argument.
22. Ermarth, *op. cit.*, p.14.
23. ibid., p.21.
24. A disjunction between theoretical claims and historical claims for the death of 'classical time', not unlike Barthes's claim for the death of the author already discussed.
25. Frank Kane, 'Dealers Couldn't Give a Forex for Politics' *Guardian* 19 September 1992, p.36.

26. ibid.
27. Martin Amis, *London Fields* (London: Penguin, 1989).
28. ibid., p.197.
29. ibid., pp.238–9.
30. Stephen Bates, 'Bewildered MPs Return in Mood of Collective Depression' *Guardian* 12 January 1994, p.2.
31. Milan Kundera, *The Book of Laughter and Forgetting* (London: Penguin, 1983), p.3.
32. Primo Levi, *'If This is a Man'* and *'The Truce'*. Translated by Stuart Woolf. With an Introduction by Paul Bailey and an Afterword by the author. (London: Abacus, 1987), pp.71–2.
33. ibid., p.123.

5. About Value

1. John Fekete, ed., *Life After Postmodernism: Essays on Value and Culture* (Basingstoke: Macmillan, 1988), p.iii.
2. Steven Connor, *Theory and Cultural Value*, (Oxford: Blackwell Publishers, 1992), p.2.
3. Anthony Appiah, 'Tolerable Falsehoods: Agency and the Interests of Theory' in Jonathon Arac and Barbara Johnson, eds, *Consequences of Theory* (Baltimore, MD: Johns Hopkins University Press, 1991). Appiah's version of the divide is between 'structure' and 'agency'. He argues that they are not competing for 'causal space' and 'truth' (what we might call 'logical explanation') but for 'narrative space', p.74.
4. Bennett, *op. cit.*
5. Norris, *op. cit.*
6. Why this should be controversial is hard to fathom, especially if my earlier point is taken that we study (are studying) 'Literature' as opposed to 'English'.
7. Bennett, *op. cit.*, pp.74–5.
8. ibid., p.120.
9. ibid., p.184, a similar account to Hunter's already mentioned.
10. ibid., p.190.
11. Easthope, *op. cit.*
12. Barbara Herrnstein Smith, *Contingencies of Value: Alternative Perspectives for Critical Theory* (Cambridge, MA: Harvard University Press, 1988).
13. Alasdair MacIntyre, *After Virtue: A Study in Moral Theory* (London: Gerald Duckworth, 1981).
14. Fekete, *op. cit.*
15. ibid., p.65.
16. Although of course the concept of a 'value' appertaining *to* an item in a metonymical chain – either *Hamlet is* the measure of great

literature or *Hamlet* is an example *of* great Literature – is no longer available.
17. Fekete, *op. cit.*, p.77.
18. *ibid.*, pp.80–1.
19. *ibid.*
20. Steven Connor, *Theory and Cultural Value*, p.2.
21. *ibid.*, p.3.
22. *ibid.*, p.2.
23. *ibid.*, p.26.
24. *ibid.*, p.27.
25. MacIntyre, *op. cit.*

PART II

6. Thanks for the Theory

1. Jan Mukarovsky, *Aesthetic Function, Norm and Value as Social Facts*. Translated from Czech, with notes and afterword by Mark E. Suino. (Ann Arbor, MI.: University of Michigan, 1979).
2. Jacques Derrida, 'Structure, Sign and Play in the Discourse of the Human Sciences' in Rick Rylance, ed., *Debating Texts: A Reader in Twentieth-Century Literary Theory and Method* (Milton Keynes: Open University Press, 1987).
3. We might go as far to substitute Science-Art and seriousness-*jouissance* for the left- and right-hand terms.
4. *The Year's Work in English Studies* 70 (1989) (Oxford: Blackwell Publishers, 1992), p.25. Ironically, *YWES* from 1994 onwards will no longer contain a part on literary theory. This will be published in a separate volume as *The Year's Work in Critical and Cultural Theory*, perhaps confirming Pinkney's fear, as well as confirming the lack of any felt necessary link between theory and the subject it is supposed to be concerned with.
5. Kevin Hart, *The Trespass of the Sign: Deconstruction, Theology and Philosophy* (Cambridge: Cambridge University Press, 1989), p.xi.
6. James Lovelock, *Gaia: The Practical Science of Planetary Medicine* (London: Gaia Books, 1991).
7. Thomas Kuhn, *The Structure of Scientific Revolutions*. 2nd edition enlarged. (Chicago: University of Chicago Press, 1970).
8. This is not to say that these categories are non-existent within the sciences, only that they are not part of the scientific imperative.
9. An example of the way science must exclude and preclude 'the unknowable' from its application is evident even in the most speculative branches such as Stephen Hawking's *A Brief History of Time* (London: Bantam Press, 1988). Carl Sagan's introduction

notes that the word that most constantly recurs in the text is 'God', in that Hawking must constantly disregard such a notion.
10. Hart, *op. cit.*, p.xi.
11. *ibid.*, p.45.
12. *ibid.*, p.211.

7. Alterity: Martin Buber's 'I-Thou' in Literature and the Arts

1. Further proof of the desire to achieve the same status for theory within the Arts as within the sciences is Giard Luce's comment that Michel de Certeau attempted 'to constitute a "science of the other"', 'Epilogue: Certeau's Heterology and the New World' *Representations* 33 (Winter 1991): 212–21, p.213.
2. Robert Young, *White Mythologies: Writing History and the West* (London: Routledge, 1990), p.19.
3. Iris M. Zavala, 'Bakhtin and Otherness: Social Heterogeneity' *Critical Studies* 2.1–2 (1990), p.77.
4. Séan Hand's introduction to Levinas's 'Otherwise Than Being' in Séan Hand, ed., *The Levinas Reader* (Oxford: Blackwell Publishers, 1989), p.88.
5. Brook Thomas, *The New Historicism and Other Old-Fashioned Topics, op. cit.*
6. Buber is put into context in greater detail further on in the chapter.
7. Martin Buber, *I and Thou*. Translated by Ronald Gregor Smith. (Edinburgh: T. & T. Clarke, 1947), pp.3–4. First published in 1923 as *Ich und Du*.

    There is a strong sense of the I-Thou in Denis Donoghue's notion of 'epireading', in Denis Donoghue, *Ferocious Alphabets* (London: Faber, 1981).

    > Epireading is not willing to leave written words as it finds them on the page, the reader wants to restore the words to a source, a human situation involving speech, character, personality, and destiny construed as having a personal form.
    >
    > We sometimes say that the reader, within this tradition, is trying to find the secret of each text, like a message lodged in a bottle floating in the sea. But it would be more accurate to say that the object of discovery is not a message or a secret but a person.

    Donoghue goes on to say 'We read to meet the other', p.99. It should be noted that Donoghue is writing in opposition to deconstruction's and Derrida's 'graphireading'.
8. The analogy between 'Literature' and 'power' in the Introduction to the book might collapse at this point, since it is unclear whether we would transform the question 'what is power?' into 'what ought power to be?' – although even here the analogy *might* hold

if we consider that changes in definitions of power have had ethical drives (or drives to exile ethics).
9. Easthope, *op. cit.*, pp.80–98.
10. Michael Theunissen, *The Other: Studies in the Social Ontology of Husserl, Heidegger, Sartre, and Buber*. Translated by Christopher Macann. Introduction by Fred R. Dallmayr. 2nd Edition. (Cambridge, MA: MIT Press, 1984).
11. *ibid.*, p.xi.
12. *ibid.*
13. For there can be no finality or mastery in the I-Thou as there is in the I-It, only the continual opening out and opening up that constitutes the relationship: even the 'play' of poststructuralism and celebratory postmodernism is not of the order of I-Thou in that it is imposed upon texts, perversely, in the same way that 'literariness' has been said to constitute Literature.
14. Hélène Cixous, 'Sorties: Out and Out: Attacks/Ways Out/Forays', in Catherine Belsey and Jane Moore, eds, *The Feminist Reader: Essays in Gender and the Politics of Literary Criticism* (Basingstoke: Macmillan, 1989).

8. Impossibility Fiction?: IF Only ...

1. Jeff Torrington, *Swing Hammer Swing!* (London: Secker and Warburg, 1992), p.23.
2. *ibid.*, p.1.
3. Ronald de Sousa, *The Rationality of Emotion* (Cambridge, MA.: MIT Press, 1987).
4. *ibid.*, p.33.
5. *ibid.*, pp.33–4.
6. See Ann Swinfen, *In Defence of Fantasy: A Study of the Genre in English and American Literature since 1945* (London: Routledge, 1984), pp.5–6, in agreement with Tolkien.
7. Jacqueline Pearson, 'Where No Man Has Gone Before: Sexual Politics and Women's Science Fiction', in Philip John Davies, ed., *Science Fiction: Social Conflict and War* (Manchester: Manchester University Press, 1990), p.16.
8. Swinfen, *op. cit.*, p.74.
9. Henry James, *The Aspern Papers* and *The Turn of the Screw* (London: Penguin, 1986); Kurt Vonnegut, *Slaughterhouse Five* (London: Triad/Panther Books, 1979); Angela Carter, *Nights at the Circus* (London: Picador, 1985).
10. Carter, *Nights at the Circus*.
11. Angela Carter, *The Infernal Desire Machines of Dr Hoffman* (London: Penguin, 1982), p.97.
12. John O. Stark, *The Literature of Exhaustion: Borges, Nabakov, and Barth* (Durham, N.C.: Duke University Press, 1974), p.1.

13. Neil Cornwell, *The Literary Fantastic: From Gothic to Postmodernism* (New York: Harvester Wheatsheaf, 1990), p.154. McHale's own term is 'the postmodern fantastic'.
14. Quoted in Cornwell, *ibid.*, p.142.

9. Despair, Enchantment, Prayer: A Conclusion

1. William Shakespeare, *The Tempest* (London: Penguin, 1968). Ed. Anne Righter (Anne Barton), p.137.
2. Joseph Heller, *Catch-22* (London: Corgi Books [Transworld Publishers Ltd], 1964), p.79.
3. Kevin Hart, *op. cit.*, p.100.
4. Helen Taylor, 'Leaving Parties and Legacies: Reflections Across the Binary Divide On a Decade of Englishes' in Bradford, *op. cit.*, p.66.
5. Ross C. Murfin, ed., *'Heart of Darkness': A Case Study in Contemporary Criticism* (New York: St. Martin's Press, 1989).

Bibliography

Amis, Martin, *London Fields* (London: Penguin, 1989).
Arac, Jonathon and Johnson, Barbara, eds, *Consequences of Theory*. Selected papers from the English Institute, 1987–88. (Baltimore, Maryland: Johns Hopkins University Press, 1991).
Barraclough, Geoffrey, *Main Trends in History*. Expanded and updated by Michael Burns. (New York: Holmes and Meier, 1991).
Barthes, Roland, *Image/Music/Text*. Essays selected and translated by Stephen Heath (London: Fontana, 1977).
—— 'The Theory of the Text' in Robert Young, ed., *Untying the Text: A Poststructuralist Reader* (London: Routledge, 1987).
Bates, Stephen, 'Bewildered MPs Return in Mood of Collective Depression' *Guardian* 12 January 1994, p.2.
Belsey, Catherine, and Moore, Jane, eds, *The Feminist Reader: Essays in Gender and the Politics of Literary Criticism* (Basingstoke: Macmillan, 1989).
Bennett, Tony, *Outside Literature* (London: Routledge, 1990).
Bradford, Richard, ed., *The State of Theory* (London: Routledge, 1993).
Buber, Martin, *I and Thou*. (1923, *Ich und Du*). Translated by Ronald Gregor Smith. (Edinburgh: T & T Clarke, 1947).
Calvino, Italo, *If on a winter's night a traveller...* (London: Picador, 1982).
Carter, Angela, *The Infernal Desire Machines of Dr Hoffman*. 1972. (London: Penguin, 1982).
—— *Nights at the Circus*. 1984. (London: Picador, 1985).
Cohen, Ralph, ed., *The Future of Literary Theory* (London: Routledge, 1989).
Connor, Steven, *Postmodernist Culture: An Introduction to Theories of the Contemporary* (Oxford: Blackwell Publishers, 1989).
—— *Theory and Cultural Value* (Oxford: Blackwell Publishers, 1992).
Cornwell, Neil, *The Literary Fantastic: From Gothic to Postmodernism* (Hemel Hempstead: Harvester Wheatsheaf, 1990).
Davies, Philip John, ed., *Science Fiction: Social Conflict and War* (Manchester: Manchester University Press, 1990).
De Man, Paul, *Blindness and Insight: Essays in the Rhetoric of Contemporary Criticism*. 2nd Edition, revised. Introduction by Wlad Godzich. (London: Methuen, 1983).
De Sousa, Ronald, *The Rationality of Emotion* (Cambridge, MA.: The MIT Press, 1987).
Derrida, Jacques, 'Structure, Sign and Play in the Discourse of the Human Sciences', in Rick Rylance, ed., *Debating Texts: A Reader in Twentieth-Century Theory and Method* (Milton Keynes: Open University Press, 1987). 123–36.
Donoghue, Denis, *Ferocious Alphabets* (London: Faber, 1981).

Earnshaw, Steven, 'Well and Truly Fact: Postmodernism in History' in Steven Earnshaw, ed., *Postmodern Surroundings* (Amsterdam: Rodopi, 1994).
Easthope, Antony, *Literary Into Cultural Studies* (London: Routledge, 1991).
Ermarth, Elizabeth Deeds, *Sequel to History: Postmodernism and the Crisis of Representational Time* (Princeton N.J.: Princeton University Press, 1992).
Fekete, John, ed., *Life After Postmodernism: Essays on Value and Culture* (Basingstoke: Macmillan, 1988).
Hand, Séan, ed., *The Levinas Reader* (Oxford: Blackwell Publishers, 1989).
Hart, Kevin, *The Trespass of the Sign: Deconstruction, Theology and Philosophy* (Cambridge: Cambridge University Press, 1989).
Hawking, Stephen W., *A Brief History of Time: From the Big Bang to Black Holes*. Introduction by Carl Sagan. (London: Bantam Press, 1988).
Heller, Joseph, *Catch-22* (London: Transworld Publishers Ltd, 1964).
Herman, Luc, Humbeeck, Kris and Lernout, Geert, eds, *(Dis)continuities: Essays on Paul de Man* (Amsterdam: Rodopi, 1989).
Hirsch Jr., E. D., *Validity in Interpretation* (New Haven: Yale University Press, 1967).
Hogan, Patrick Colm, *The Politics of Interpretation: Ideology, Professionalism, and the Study of Literature* (New York: Oxford University Press, 1990).
Holub, Robert C., *Reception Theory: A Critical Introduction* (London: Methuen, 1984).
Hunter, Ian, *Culture and Government: The Emergence of Literary Education* (Basingstoke: Macmillan, 1988).
Hutcheon, Linda, *A Poetics of Postmodernism* (London: Routledge, 1988).
James, Henry, *The Aspern Papers* and *The Turn of the Screw* (London: Penguin, 1986).
Kane, Frank, 'Dealers Couldn't Give a Forex for Politics', *Guardian* 19 September 1992, p.36.
Kirwan, James, *Literature, Rhetoric, Metaphysics: Literary Theory and Literary Aesthetics* (London: Routledge, 1990).
Knapp, Steven and Michaels, Walter Benn, 'Against Theory' *Critical Inquiry* 8 (1982): 723–42.
—— 'A Reply to Our Critics' *Critical Inquiry* 9 (1982–83), 790–800.
Kuhn, Thomas S., *The Structure of Scientific Revolutions*. 2nd edition enlarged. (Chicago: University of Chicago Press, 1970).
Kundera, Milan, *The Book of Laughter and Forgetting* (London: Penguin, 1983).
Lehman, David, *Signs of the Times: Deconstruction and the Fall of Paul de Man* (London: André Deutsch, 1991).
Levi, Primo, *'If This Is a Man' and 'The Truce'*. Translated by Stuart Woolf. With an Introduction by Paul Bailey and an Afterword by the author. (London: Abacus, 1987).
Lovelock, James, *Gaia: The Practical Science of Planetary Medicine* (London: Gaia Books Ltd., 1991).

Luce, Giard, 'Epilogue: Michel de Certeau's Heterology and the New World', *Representations* 33 (Winter 1991), 212–21.

Lyotard, Jean-François, *The Postmodern Condition: A Report on Knowledge*. Translated by Geoff Bennington and Brian Massumi. Foreword by Fredric Jameson. (Manchester: Manchester University Press, 1984).

MacIntyre, Alasdair, *After Virtue: A Study in Moral Theory* (London: Gerald Duckworth, 1981).

McGann, Jerome J., *Social Values and Poetic Acts: The Historical Judgement of Literary Work* (Massachusetts: Harvard University Press, 1988).

McHale, Brian, *Postmodernist Fiction* (London: Methuen, 1987).

Mitchell, W. J. T., ed., *Against Theory: Literary Studies and the New Pragmatism* (Chicago: University of Chicago Press, 1985).

Mukarovsky, Jan, *Aesthetic Function, Norm and Value as Social Facts*. Translated from Czech, with notes and afterword by Mark E. Suino. (Ann Arbor, Michigan: University of Michigan, 1979).

'Murder Case Man's "Threat" to Shoot Teddy Bears', *Guardian* 11 March 1992, p.2.

Murfin, Ross C., ed., *'Heart of Darkness': A Case Study in Contemporary Criticism* (New York: St. Martin's Press, 1989).

Nietzsche, Friedrich, *'The Birth of Tragedy' and 'The Genealogy of Morals'*. Translated by Francis Golffing. (New York: Anchor Press, 1956).

Norris, Christopher, *What's Wrong With Postmodernism: Critical Theory and the Ends of Philosophy* (Hemel Hemptead: Harvester Wheatsheaf, 1990).

Pinkney, Tony, *The Year's Work in English Studies* 70 (1989) (Oxford: Blackwell Publishers, 1992).

Pynchon, Thomas, *Gravity's Rainbow*. 1973. (London: Picador, 1975).

Rabinow, Paul, *The Foucault Reader* (London: Penguin, 1986).

Ray, William, *Literary Meaning: From Phenomenology to Deconstruction* (Oxford: Basil Blackwell, 1984).

Rigney, Ann, 'Review of Lionel Gossman's *Literature and History*', *History and Theory* 31.2 (1992), 208–22.

Ross, Andrew, ed., *Universal Abandon? – The Politics of Postmodernism* (Minneapolis: University of Minnesota Press, 1989).

Shakespeare, William, *The Tempest*. Ed. Anne Righter (Anne Barton). (London: Penguin, 1968).

Siegel, Jules, 'Who is Thomas Pynchon ... and Why Did He Take Off with My Wife?', *Playboy* 34 (March 1977), 97, 122, 168–70, 172, 174.

Small, Ian and Guy, Josephine, 'English in Crisis (2)', *Essays in English* 40.3 (1990), 185–97.

Smith, Barbara Herrnstein, *Contingencies of Value: Alternative Perspectives for Critical Theory* (Cambridge, MA.: Harvard University Press, 1988).

Stark, John O., *The Literature of Exhaustion: Borges, Nabakov, and Barth* (Durham, N.C.: Duke University Press, 1974).

Steiner, Peter, ed., *The Prague School: Selected Writings, 1929–1946* (Austin: University of Texas, 1982).

Swinfen, Ann, *In Defence of Fantasy: A Study of the Genre in English and American Literature since 1945* (London: Routledge, 1984).

Tallis, Raymond, *Not Saussure: A Critique of Post-Saussurean Literary Theory* (Basingstoke: Macmillan, 1988).

Theunissen, Michael, *The Other: Studies in the Social Ontology of Husserl, Heidegger, Sartre, and Buber*. Translated by Christopher Macann. Introduction by Fred R. Dallmayr. 2nd edition. (Cambridge, MA.: MIT Press, 1984).

Thomas, Brook, *The New Historicism and Other Old-Fashioned Topics* (Princeton, N.J.: Princeton University Press, 1991).

Torrington, Jeff, *Swing Hammer Swing!* (London: Secker and Warburg, 1992).

Veeser, H. Aram, ed., *The New Historicism* (London: Routledge, 1989).

Vonnegut, Kurt, *Slaughterhouse Five* (London: Triad/Panther Books, 1979).

Weisenberger, Steven, *A 'Gravity's Rainbow' Companion: Sources and Contexts for Pynchon's Novel* (Athens: University of Georgia Press, 1988).

Wimsatt, W. K. R., Jr, and Beardsley, M., *The Verbal Icon: Studies in the Meaning of Poetry* (Kentucky: University of Kentucky Press, 1954).

Young, Robert, *White Mythologies: Writing History and the West* (London: Routledge, 1990).

Zavala, Iris M., 'Bakhtin and Otherness: Social Heterogeneity', *Critical Studies* 2.1–2 (1990), 77–89.

Special Issues

New German Critique 22 (Winter 1981), 'Modernism'.
New German Critique 33 (Fall 1984), 'Modernity and Postmodernity'.

Index

academia, 1, 115, 121, 150, 153, 155, 158
  see also higher education
aesthetic entity, 46–50
aesthetics, 1, 6, 11, 14, 85–90, 92, 97, 98, 108, 121
alterity, 62, 119–34
alternative-world fiction, 136, 145
Amis, Martin, *London Fields*, 76–7
anthropological universal given, 97, 99, 108, 120, 126, 152
Appiah, Anthony, 84
approaches, *see* theory
argumentation of book, 2–3, 82–3, 107
art and the arts, 8, 11–12, 97, 98, 108, 111–14, 115–17, 119–34, 150, 159
audience, *see* reader, the
author, 3, 15, 21–35, 53, 57, 159
  as auteur, 25
  as creator, 26–8, 33, 129, 141, 156
  death of, 21–35
  as god, 28–9
  and intention, 39–44, 128, 159
  varieties of, 54, 57, 130
  as opposed to writer, 30–35
author function, 31–5

Bakhtin, Mikhail, 26, 114, 119–20, 151
Barth, John, 147
Barthes, Roland, 10, 21–28, 30, 32, 34–5, 40, 152
Baudrillard, Jean, 77
Beardsley, M., 38–41, 43–6, 51, 53–4
belief, as opposed to theory, 14, 60
Bennett, Tony, 6, 55, 85–92, 157
Book of Laughter and Forgetting, The, 78
Borges, Jorge Luis, 147, 148

'bricks in the Tate', 127, 153
Buber, Martin, 119–34, 151
Burroughs, Edgar Rice, 124–5

Calvino, Italo, 21, 147, 148–9
canon, 4, 90–1
Carter, Angela, *The Infernal Desire Machines of Dr Hoffman*, 146
  Nights at the Circus, 145–6
Cartland, Barbara, 78
chaos theory, 8n12, 114–15
citations, 113–14
Cixous, Hélène, 133
Colomb, Gregory G., 37n3
Connor, Steven, 15, 60–1, 82–3, 98–100
Conrad, Joseph, 148
copyright, 25, 29–30
Cornwell, Neil, 147
criticism, *see* theory
Culler, Jonathan, 23
cultural materialism, 120
cultural studies, 9, 55, 133, 157
cyberpunk, 142

de Certeau, Michel, 119n1, 151
deconstruction, *see under* theory
de Man, Paul, 10, 12n19, 22–3, 26, 29, 30, 33–5, 41–2, 44–50, 51, 53–4, 59–60, 100, 125, 127–8, 129, 152
depthlessness, *see under* postmodernism
Derrida, Jacques, 23, 29, 108, 110, 117–18, 120, 125, 133, 151
  see also theory: deconstruction
de Saussure, Ferdinand, 1–2, 24
de Sousa, Ronald, 139–41
dialogicalism, 126
dialogicians, 125
dialogism, 114, 120
  see also Bakhtin

disciplinary collapse, 67–8
Docherty, Thomas, 61–2
Donoghue, Denis, 123n7

$E=mc^2$, 83–4
Easthope, Antony, 4n3, 55, 92–4, 124–5
education, 1, 6, 11–12, 15, 16, 109–110, 133, 153–8
    see also English Studies; literary studies
emergence, 139–42
emotions, 8
    see also literature: affective nature
English Studies, 1, 11–12, 15, 55, 57, 94, 154, 156–8
    see also education; literary studies
epi-reading, 123n7
epistemology, 6–8, 10
Ermarth, Elizabeth Deeds, 63, 72–4
ethical grounding, as opposed to theoretical, 78–80, 99–100, 104
ethics, 1, 78–80, 117, 120, 121, 125, 151, 159
evaluation, 39–41, 42, 82–104, 113, 159
    see also value
evidence, in theory, 36–41, 43, 54, 129
existential philosophy, 125–7

facts, see under value; see also truth
Fekete, John, 94–8
fiction, nature of, see impossibility fiction
Fish, Stanley, 10, 60
Formalism, see under theory
Foster, Hal, 61
Foucault, Michel, 29–35, 62, 86, 113, 120
freedom, as grounding, 99, 151
free indirect discourse, 148

Frow, John, 86
Frye, Northrop, 46

Gaia, 114
gender, 1, 152
God, as an absolute, 83–4, 117n9, 127
Gossman, Lionel, 68
graphireading, 123n7
Gravity's Rainbow, 65–7, 70–2
Guy, Josephine, 16

Hare, R. M., 155
Hart, Kevin, 110, 117–18, 155n3
Hartmann, Geoffrey, 23
Hawkings, Stephen, 117n9
Heidegger, Martin, 49, 100, 122, 125–6
hermeneutic circle, 26, 48–50
hermeneutics, 26, 37–8, 50, 82, 108, 121, 128
    see also meaning
higher education, 1, 15, 89–90, 109–110, 156–7
    see also education
Hirsch, E. D. Jr, 5, 21–2, 38, 41–5, 51, 53–4, 116, 128, 129–30
historiographic metafiction, 67n17
history, 59–81
    as discourse, 65
    end of, 22, 59–81
    ethical foundation, 78–80, 152
    as fiction, 67–8
    grounding, 79
    and legitimation, 65–8, 75–6
    and metanarrative, 62–4, 76
    and micronarratives, 62, 65
    and narrative, 7, 61–3, 67, 70–6, 79–80
    paradigms of, 65–74
    and postmodernism, 59–81
    as a science, 75–6
    and teleology, 61
    and time, 70–4, 76–7
Hogan, Patrick Colm, 28–9
holocaust, 66n14, 72, 79–80

Index

human condition, the, 156, 158
Hunter, Ian, 11–12, 87
Husserl, Edmund, 122, 125–6
Hutcheon, Linda, 67n17
Huyssen, Andreas, 61

I-It, 119–134
I-Thou, 119–34, 135–6, 151, 156, 157, 159
ideological grounding, as opposed to theoretical grounding, 32
ideology, 11, 17, 154
If This Is a Man, 79–80
imagination, 8, 128–9, 133, 157, 159
imaging, 8
impossibility fiction, 135–49, 160–1
   and emergence, 139–42
   and fantasy, 142–3
   and the ineffable, 143–9
   as invisible, 147–8
   as 'magic', 137–49
   metaphor as, 136–43, 146
   and science-fiction, 139–42, 144–5
Infernal Desire Machines of Dr Hoffman, The, 146
intention, 3, 15, 21, 28, 36–57, 127–8, 129
intentional fallacy, 38–41, 42, 44–6
intentionality, 45–50, 127–8
   see also intention
interpretation, 28, 38, 40–4, 48–50
   see also hermeneutics; meaning
intersubjectivity, 126
irrationality, 152, 158
irony, 10, 130, 152

James, Henry, 148
   The Turn of the Screw, 143–4, 145
Jameson, Fredric, 60–1, 62
Jauss, Hans Robert, 14, 89
jouissance, 10, 152
Joyce, James, 148

Keneally, Thomas, 79
Kirwan, James, 4–6
Knapp, Steven, 12n19, 50–4, 56, 130
   see also theory: neopragmatist
Kuhn, T. S., 14, 115
Kundera, Milan, *The Book of Laughter and Forgetting*, 78

Larkin, Philip, 22, 23n6, 30
Lehman, David, 9–10, 33–4
Leicester University, 157
Lentricchia, Frank, 34n27
Levi, Primo, *If This Is a Man*, 79–80
Levinas, Immanuel, 120, 125, 126, 151
literariness, 17, 112, 130–1, 149
Literature
   and the aesthetic, 87–90, 91–2
   affective nature, 128, 157
   and authenticity, 125, 126, 132
   as 'blik', 155
   as cultural product, 92–4, 152
   definition of, 3–9, 11–12, 14–17, 97, 107, 113, 115, 123–34, 148, 150–6 *see also* literature: grounding
   and elitism, 89, 92, 93, 124–5
   as enjoyment, 154–6
   and ethics, 132, 151, 159
   of exhaustion, 147
   grounding of, 57–8, 84–94, 102, 132, 150–9 *see also* literature: definition of
   and I-Thou, 123–34
   as an ideological tool, 55, 85–94
   and immediacy, 124–5
   and intention, 55–6
   and interdisciplinarity, 133
   interpretation of, 38, 55–6
   see also meaning; hermeneutics
   and pedagogy, 89–92, 102
   see also education
   philosophy of, 115, 134, 151, 159

Literature – *continued*
  as special practice, 86–9, 92
  as text, 92–3
  and value, 82–3, 91–2, 96, 154–9
  literary studies, 1, 9, 55, 154–6
  literary understanding, 93
  see also English Studies
London Fields, 76–7
Lovelock, James, 114
Luce, Giard, 119n1
Lyotard, Jean-François, 62, 65

MacIntyre, Alasdair, 94, 100–1
magical realism, 145–6
Major, John, 78
male authority, 28–9
Marquez, Gabriel Garcia, 148
McGann, Jerome J., 14, 62n7, 120
McHale, Brian, 66–8, 147
meaning, 10, 12, 13, 21, 23, 26, 28–9, 31–5, 36–44, 48–52, 82, 86
  see also interpretation; hermeneutics
Mehlman, Jeffrey, 23n5
metanarratives, *see under* postmodernism
metaphor, 6, 136–43
methodology, *see* theory
Michaels, Walter Benn, 12n19, 50–4, 56, 130
  see also theory: neopragmatist
Miller, J. Hillis, 23
Mink, Louis, 101
Mitchell, W. J. T., 51
moral grounding, as opposed to theoretical grounding, 28–9, 31, 32
Mukarovsky, Jan, 48n30, 88, 107–8
mysticism, 117–18, 122, 152, 153

Nabakov, Vladimir, 147
narrative, as grounding, 100–1
nation state, 63–4, 74
neopragmatism, *see under* theory
New Historicism, *see under* theory

Nights at the Circus, 145–6
Nietzsche, Friedrich, 3, 8, 125
Norris, Christopher, 7, 85

objectivity, 3, 7, 72, 75
  see also truth
originality, 27
otherness, *see* alterity

paradigm shifts, 115
parallel-world fiction, 142–6
Parrinder, Patrick, 1, 147
Pearson, Jacqueline, 141–2
pedagogy, *see* education
perception, 8
phallogocentrism, 28–9
phenomenology, 10, 107, 122, 126
philosophy, 117–18
  antifoundational, 117, 134
  and mysticism, 117–18
  as non-rational, 130, 133
  as opposed to theory, 117–18, 121, 130
Pinkney, Tony, 110, 154
pleasure, 12
pluralism, 15–16
poetics, 13, 14, 50
political correctness, 79, 120, 151–2
politics, 1, 78
popular culture, 4
  see also cultural studies
portmanteau novel, 147
postmodern age, 28, 35, 60, 63, 68, 71, 76, 78–81, 151
postmodern fiction, 65–8, 78, 145–7
postmodernism, 3, 7, 15, 16, 75–7, 78–9
  as ahistorical, 62, 80
  and antifoundationalism, 61, 67, 80 *see also* theory: neo-pragmatist
  collapse of disciplines, 67–8
  and context, 69–70, 71–2
  and critical space, 60
  and depthlessness, 61, 63, 74

postmodernism – *continued*
   as end of history, 60–3, 71, 76, 77
   and history, 59–81
   and metanarratives, 60, 62, 63–7, 71, 85
   and New Historicism, 62–3, 71
   and particularity, 61–3, 75
   and pluralism, 66, 86
   and relativism, 65–7, 79, 85, 86
   and self-consciousness, 59–62, 69–70
   self-exempting, 61, 69, 81
   status of, 59–81
   and time, 60, 70–4
pragmatism, *see under* theory
Prague Linguistic School, 44n20, 88
   see also Mukarovsky, Jan
psychology, 1
Pynchon, Thomas, 33–5, 148
   Gravity's Rainbow, 65–7, 70–2

race, 1
rationality, 75, 152, 158
   see also objectivity
Ray, William, 8, 10, 11, 12n19, 13, 103
reader, the, 50, 123–34
reading experience, the, 121, 135–7, 149, 154, 156–9
relativism, *see under* postmodernism
responsibility, 29, 66–7, 79, 151
Rigney, Ann, 68n19
Rorty, Richard, 61
Russ, Joanna, 142

Sartre, Jean-Paul, 8–9, 126
science fiction, 139–42
Second World War, 65–7, 71–2
semiotic systems, 4
Shakespeare, William, *The Tempest*, 158
Siegel, Jules, 33
simulacra, 77
Slaughterhouse Five, 144–5
Small, Ian, 16

Smith, Barbara Herrnstein, 94, 99, 100, 101
society, 22
Spivak, Gayatri Chakravorty, 117
Stark, John, 147
students, 1, 8, 57, 90, 102, 109–110, 156–7
supplements, 117
Swinfen, Ann, 142–3
Swing Hammer Swing!, 138–9

Tallis, Raymond, 7, 29
Taylor, Helen, 156–7
text, the, 2, 7, 9–10, 44–50, 68–9
textuality, 68–9
theory
   antifoundational, 7, 134, 150–2, 158, 159 *see also under* postmodernism; *see also* theory: neopragmatism
   author-centred, 2, 21–35, 54, 156 *see also* author
   biographical, *see* theory: author-centred; author
   contextual, *see* theory: extrinsic; theory: sociohistorical
   contingency-based, 12 *see also* theory: sociohistorical
   deconstruction, 9, 10, 23, 29, 33, 54, 68–9, 85–6, 110, 114, 116, 117–18, 119–20, 129, 132
   end of, 59–60
   extrinsic, 1–2, 22, 26 *see also* theory: sociohistorical
   feminist, 2, 17, 28–9, 119, 130, 157
   formalist, 1, 2, 14, 22, 28, 58, 110, 149, 157
   grounding of, 3, 6–8, 12, 16, 24, 41, 54–5, 57–8, 85, 101–2, 107–20, 150–9
   hermeneutic, *see* hermeneutics
   history of, 1–2, 101, 108, 112, 157
   immanence-based, 2, 10, 12, 14, 15, 17, 21–5, 33, 35, 40, 43–50, 77, 107, 116, 119, 129–32, 150 *compare* theory: sociohistorical

theory – *continued*
  intrinsic, 1–2 *see also* theory: immanence-based
  liberal-humanist, 15, 17, 49n33, 158
  marxist, 2, 17, 54, 85–92, 93–4, 110, 130
  neopragmatist, 16, 110–11, 130, 158 *see also* theory: antifoundational; Knapp, Steven
  New Critical, 21, 39, 41, 44–50, 156 *see also* Beardsley
  New Historicist, 62–3, 120, 130, 156, 157
  non-rational, 3, 152 *see also* mysticism; theory: antifoundational
  pluralist, 15
  political, 17 *see also* theory: feminist; theory: Marxist
  post-marxist, 6, 85–92, 93–4
  postcolonial, 119
  postmodern, 59–81, 83, 85–6, 101, 114, 119, 122, 150–2
  poststructuralist, 2, 4, 7, 8, 10, 15, 22, 23, 28, 29, 34, 68–9, 85, 110, 119–120 *see also* theory: deconstruction
  pragmatist, 7, 60, 153 *see also* theory: neopragmatist
  psychoanalytical, 54, 120, 130
  reader-response, 108 *see also* theory: reception history
  reception history, 14, 88–9
  and science, 110–17
  sociohistorical, 2, 10, 14, 15, 17, 22, 34, 35, 85–92, 103, 107, 116, 119, 129–30, 150, 153 *compare* theory: immanence-based
  structuralist, 2, 10, 22, 23, 107–8, 120, 157
  text-based, *see* theory: immanence-based
  transcendental, 10 *see also* theory: immanence-based
  see also aesthetics; hermeneutics; poetics
Theunissen, Michael, 125
thick description, *see* theory: New Historicist
Thomas, Brook, 62n7, 120
Torrington, Jeff, *Swing Hammer Swing!*, 138–9
truth, 29, 30, 65–7, 85–6, 112, 136, 148, 153
Turn of the Screw, The, 143–4, 145
Turner, Mark, 37n3

value, 1, 3, 10, 12, 15, 82–104
  absolute, 82, 83, 97–8, 99
  aesthetic, 89–90, 98, 100
  commodity conception of, 95–6
  of enjoyment, 154–5
  ethical, 100
  exile of, 101
  and facts, 83–4
  grounding of, 96–8
  as limit of theory, 102
  and literature, 95–7, 154–9
  as regulatory system, 95–9
  relative, 82, 99
  and relativism, 86
Veeser, H. Aram, 62
voice, 23–8
Voloshinov, V. N., 2, 24
Vonnegut, Kurt, *Slaughterhouse Five*, 144–5

Warren, Austin, 1
Weisenberger, Steven, 33
Wellek, René, 1
White, Hayden, 101
Williams, Raymond, 120
Wimsatt, W. K. R., 38–41, 43–6, 51, 53–4
Woolf, Virginia, 148
writer, the, as opposed to the author, 30–5
writing, 24–8

Young, Robert, 119

Zavala, Iris M., 119–20